The Entrepreneurial Mindset:

How to Think Like a Successful Business Owner

I0479419

FIRST EDITION

Dr. Lila K. Whitaker

Publisher's Note

The information contained within this book is based on the author's research, experiences, and opinions. The author and publisher have made every effort to ensure accuracy and completeness, but make no warranties or guarantees regarding the information provided. Readers are encouraged to exercise their own judgment and seek professional advice where necessary. The publisher, author, and any other involved parties cannot be held liable for any errors or omissions in the content.

First published in the United States in 2023 by ByteWise Publishing.

© 2023 Bytewise Publishing, 188 Grand St Fl 2 New York, NY 10013.

ISBNs

Kindle edition	N/A
Paperback edition	9798388325310

THIS PAGE IS INTENTIONALLY LEFT BLANK

Table of Contents

Identifying and Analyzing Market Opportunities 71

Developing a Business Plan 90

Implementing Effective Marketing Strategies 152

Overcoming Obstacles and Challenges 175

Putting it All Together: Applying the Entrepreneurial Mindset   *195*

About the author

Dr. Lila K. Whitaker is a renowned entrepreneur, business strategist, and author with over 20 years of experience in fostering entrepreneurial success. She holds a Ph.D. in Organizational Psychology and a Master's in Business Administration, specializing in entrepreneurship. Dr. Whitaker has worked with numerous startups and established businesses, helping them develop and implement innovative strategies to thrive in competitive markets. She is also a sought-after keynote speaker at conferences and corporate events, sharing her insights on entrepreneurial mindset and business growth.

THIS PAGE IS INTENTIONALLY LEFT BLANK

Introduction to the Entrepreneurial Mindset

Understanding the Entrepreneurial Mindset

Definition of Entrepreneurship

Entrepreneurship has become a buzzword in today's world, with many people aspiring to start their own businesses. But what is entrepreneurship, and what does it truly mean to be an entrepreneur?

At its core, entrepreneurship is the process of identifying a problem or opportunity and creating a solution or product that meets the needs of customers. It involves taking calculated risks, being innovative, and constantly adapting to changing market conditions.

Entrepreneurs are not just business owners; they are individuals who possess a particular mindset that enables them to see opportunities where others may only see problems. They are passionate, determined, and willing to take risks to achieve their goals.

This mindset is essential in today's fast-paced, constantly evolving business landscape, where innovation and agility are key to success. Without this entrepreneurial mindset, it can be difficult to develop new ideas, build innovative products, and create sustainable businesses.

In the following sections, we will explore the role of

mindset in entrepreneurship, the journey of an entrepreneur, and the characteristics that are essential for success in this field. By understanding the entrepreneurial mindset, you can gain the knowledge and tools to build a successful business and achieve your entrepreneurial goals.

Characteristics of Entrepreneurs

Successful entrepreneurs possess certain characteristics that set them apart from the rest. These characteristics include:

Passion - Entrepreneurs are passionate about their work, and they have a strong desire to make a difference in the world.

Resilience - Entrepreneurs face many challenges and setbacks, but they have the ability to bounce back from these obstacles and keep moving forward.

Creativity - Entrepreneurs are always thinking outside the box and coming up with innovative solutions to problems.

Risk-taking - Entrepreneurs are willing to take calculated risks in order to achieve their goals.

Flexibility - Entrepreneurs are adaptable and able to pivot when necessary to adjust to changing circumstances.

Perseverance - Entrepreneurs are determined and persistent in the pursuit of their goals.

Entrepreneurship is not for everyone, but if you possess these characteristics and are willing to put in the hard work, you too can think like a successful business owner.

Benefits of Developing an Entrepreneurial Mindset

In today's fast-paced world, it's becoming increasingly essential to cultivate an entrepreneurial mindset. With the constant disruption in business, it's critical to have this mindset because it empowers individuals to progress in the face of change, seize opportunities, and create value in the market.

Developing an entrepreneurial mindset offers several benefits. Firstly, it enables individuals to think creatively and outside the box, allowing them to come up with innovative solutions to complex problems. Secondly, it encourages individuals to take calculated risks, helping them to push past their comfort zones and take dynamic actions. Thirdly, it fosters a growth mindset, which is critical to attaining long-term success. By acknowledging failures, learning from setbacks, and embracing a growth mindset, individuals can grow and evolve as business owners.

Moreover, an entrepreneurial mindset enables individuals to develop more profound and more meaningful connections with the people they serve. They can build strong relationships by focusing on customer needs, understanding the pulse of the market, and communicating efficiently with their team, investors, and stakeholders.

Finally, an entrepreneurial mindset enables individuals to be more fulfilled and happy in their personal and professional lives. They become driven, motivated, and passionate about their work, focusing on what makes them happy rather than just pursuing financial gain.

Developing an entrepreneurial mindset is critical, no matter what stage you're at in business. It helps to unlock creativity, fosters growth, allows for meaningful connections, and can ultimately lead to greater fulfillment and happiness.

Importance of Entrepreneurial Thinking

Entrepreneurial thinking is the foundation of any successful business venture. It requires an innovative and dynamic approach to problem-solving, decision-making, and risk-taking. The ability to see opportunities where others don't, identify gaps in the market, and create innovative solutions to fill them is what sets entrepreneurs apart.

Adopting an entrepreneurial mindset means embracing a mindset of growth, learning, and resilience. It is about being proactive, taking ownership of challenges, and seeking opportunities to learn from failures. As an entrepreneur, it is essential to be open to new ideas, flexible in your approach, and willing to take calculated risks to enhance your chances of success.

The entrepreneurial mindset is also characterized by a fundamental understanding of the importance of customer-centricity, adaptability, and agility. To succeed, entrepreneurs must develop a deep understanding of the needs and wants of their target customers and be able to pivot their strategies quickly in response to market changes, consumer behavior, and emerging trends.

The importance of entrepreneurial thinking cannot be overstated. Developing an entrepreneurial mindset is the first step towards building a successful business that can thrive in today's fast-paced, ever-changing, and competitive business landscape. By cultivating the right mindset, individuals and teams can unlock their full potential, overcome challenges, and achieve their entrepreneurial dreams.

Challenges of Entrepreneurship

Entrepreneurship is an adventurous journey, but it's not for everyone. The challenges you'll face require a lot of mental and emotional stamina, and your resilience will be tested several times throughout the journey.

One of the primary challenges that entrepreneurs face is uncertainty. The future is never certain, and you'll constantly be met with unexpected obstacles that can throw you off balance. The market dynamics may change, and competitors may enter or leave the market, affecting your business's viability.

Another major challenge is managing risk. All entrepreneurs must take calculated risks, but this comes with a lot of pressure. You'll have to learn how to weigh the risks and rewards of every decision you make and manage the potential fallout when things don't go as planned.

The pressure to manage finances is another challenge that can deter many entrepreneurs. At the early stages of your business, cash flow might be irregular, and you may have to bear personal financial burdens until the business picks up. This can create a lot of stress and financial pressure.

The entrepreneurial journey is also a lonely one, and you may have to face many difficult decisions alone. As the leader of the business, you're responsible for guiding the team towards the business goals, and at times, you might have to make unpopular decisions that can affect your relationships with your team.

Entrepreneurship is a rewarding journey that requires a strong mindset and the ability to face challenges head-on. The challenges you face will determine your success, and the ability to manage them successfully will determine your business's longevity.

The Role of Mindset in Entrepreneurship

Growth Mindset

As an entrepreneur, your mindset is essentially your personal stance on business and what you're willing to do to achieve success. Mindset plays a critical role in shaping the way entrepreneurs react to challenges, capitalise on opportunities, and approach their work in general. In fact, the entrepreneurial mindset can ultimately determine the difference between success and failure in business.

There are two types of mindsets: fixed and growth. A fixed mindset assumes that intelligence and abilities are static, whereas a growth mindset believes that one's intelligence and abilities can be developed and improved over time through hard work and dedication.

Those with a fixed mindset may be hesitant to take risks because they don't want to fail and be seen as incompetent. On the other hand, those with a growth mindset embrace challenges and view them as opportunities for growth and learning.

It's important for entrepreneurs to have a growth mindset as it allows for flexibility, adaptation to market changes, and innovation. Possessing a growth mindset means that entrepreneurs are not afraid to pivot when necessary and will continuously seek out resources and knowledge to improve their skills and business operations.

In contrast, those with a fixed mindset may struggle to adapt to changes in the market, may be reluctant to seek feedback and may be hesitant to invest in their businesses.

In essence, the key to developing an entrepreneurial mindset is to recognise that setbacks and failures are opportunities for growth and learning, and to view challenges as a motivational force for problem-solving and innovation. A growth mindset means continuous learning, embracing discomfort, and being open to new opportunities. By adopting a growth mindset and focusing on personal development, entrepreneurs can steer their businesses in a direction that leads to long-term success.

Why Mindset Matters for Entrepreneurs

Entrepreneurship is not an easy path. It is full of challenges, uncertainties, and risks. Starting and growing a successful business takes more than just a good idea or a sound strategy. It requires an entrepreneurial mindset, which is the way of thinking, behaving, and approaching problems that distinguishes successful entrepreneurs from others.

Why does mindset matter for entrepreneurs? The simple answer is that the mindset of an entrepreneur determines how he or she reacts to the challenges, setbacks, and opportunities that arise in the course of the business journey. It shapes his or her attitudes, beliefs, and habits, and influences his or her decisions and actions.

Entrepreneurship is not a one-time event but a continuous journey that demands a growth-oriented mindset. As an entrepreneur, you need to be open-minded, flexible, and adaptable to changing circumstances. You need to embrace failures, learn from mistakes, and persist in the face of obstacles. You need to have a passion for your business, a sense of purpose, and a clear vision of your goals and values.

The entrepreneurial mindset is not something you are born with, but something you can develop and cultivate. It requires a conscious effort to break free from limiting beliefs, negative self-talk, and fear of failure. It requires a willingness to take calculated risks, step out of your comfort zone, and seek feedback and support from others.

In the next section, we will explore the key elements of the entrepreneurial mindset and how they can help you build a successful business.

How to Develop a Growth Mindset

In order to succeed as an entrepreneur, it is important to develop a growth mindset. This means having a belief in your ability to improve and learn from your mistakes. Whether you are just starting out or have been in business for years, it is never too late to adopt a growth mindset.

One way to develop a growth mindset is to embrace failure as an opportunity for growth. Instead of seeing failure as a sign of inadequacy, successful entrepreneurs view it as a valuable learning experience. By reframing failure in this way, you can use setbacks as an opportunity to learn from your mistakes and make improvements for the future.

Another way to develop a growth mindset is to focus on your strengths instead of your weaknesses. While it is important to acknowledge areas where you can improve, it is equally important to recognize your strengths and leverage them to achieve success. By focusing on what you do well, you can build on your strengths and create a business that is uniquely suited to your skills and abilities.

Finally, developing a growth mindset requires a willingness to take risks and embrace change. Successful entrepreneurs understand that innovation and growth require a willingness to step outside of your comfort zone and take calculated risks. By being open to new ideas and approaches, you can stay ahead of the curve and capitalize on emerging opportunities.

Developing a growth mindset is essential for success as an entrepreneur. By embracing failure, focusing on your strengths, and taking risks, you can cultivate a mindset that is poised for growth and success in the business world.

Importance of Mindset Development

In order to become a successful entrepreneur, it is essential to develop and maintain the right mindset. The way you think and approach your business and life can significantly impact your success. Developing an entrepreneurial mindset is not something that happens overnight; it requires dedication and persistence in the pursuit of your goals.

The importance of mindset development can be seen in the lives of successful entrepreneurs. They possess a mindset that allows them to see opportunities where others see challenges, and to persevere through difficult times. Their mindset is centered around innovation, risk-taking, and a focus on growth and improvement.

For an entrepreneur, the right mindset can be the difference between success and failure. It can make all the difference in the crucial decision-making processes and in overcoming obstacles. A positive and proactive mindset can help entrepreneurs navigate the challenges of starting and growing a business.

Developing a growth mindset is one of the essential aspects of the entrepreneurial mindset. This means being open to learning, experimentation, and feedback. It requires a willingness to take risks, make mistakes, and embrace failure as part of the learning process.

Having the right mindset is a critical aspect of entrepreneurship. Develop a growth mindset that is open to learning and experimentation, and be willing to take risks and embrace failures. With the right mindset, you can overcome the challenges of starting and growing a successful business.

Mindset Strategies for Entrepreneurs

SECTION: The Role of Mindset in Entrepreneurship

SUBSECTION: Mindset Strategies for Entrepreneurs

Entrepreneurship is challenging, and success in this area depends on developing a specific type of mindset. This section focuses on the mindset strategies that entrepreneurs must master to succeed in their businesses.

Self-Awareness:
Self-awareness is a crucial aspect of developing the entrepreneurial mindset. Knowing yourself inside out provides insight into your weaknesses, strengths, values, and beliefs, enabling you to align your actions with your

core beliefs.

Growth Mindset:
Entrepreneurs must have a growth mindset, which is the belief that they can learn, improve and develop their skills with time. A growth mindset allows entrepreneurs to focus on their learning process and development rather than the end goal. This perspective helps entrepreneurs stay motivated throughout the challenging journey from ideation to realization.

Risk-Taking:
Taking risks is an essential part of entrepreneurship. Entrepreneurs need to develop the ability to take calculated risks that align with their vision and values. Taking risks leads to growth, learning, and development for entrepreneurs.

Perseverance:
Entrepreneurship is not a straight path; it is full of twists, turns, and setbacks. Perseverance is the ability to overcome these obstacles continuously. Entrepreneurs must learn to be tenacious and persistent to achieve their goals and overcome the hurdles that come in their way.

Adaptability:
Entrepreneurs must be adaptable, as businesses operate in a dynamic environment. They must be flexible and pivot when necessary to keep up with the changing demands of their customers and the industry.

Conclusion:
Developing and mastering the entrepreneurial mindset takes time, effort and dedication. By cultivating self-awareness, adopting a growth mindset, taking calculated risks, exhibiting perseverance and adaptability,

entrepreneurs can set themselves up for success in their entrepreneurial journeys.

The Journey of an Entrepreneur

Understanding the Entrepreneurial Journey

Entrepreneurship is a journey, not just a destination. It's a continuous process of trial and error, success and failure, and learning and growing. The journey of an entrepreneur begins with an idea, a passion, and a vision. Successful entrepreneurs understand that the journey won't be easy, and there will be obstacles and challenges to overcome.

To understand the journey of an entrepreneur, it's essential to know that it's not a linear path. There isn't a one-size-fits-all solution, and each entrepreneur's journey will be unique. Some entrepreneurs start with a small business, while others begin with a side hustle. However, there are common stages that most entrepreneurs will go through.

The first stage of the entrepreneurial journey is the ideation stage. It's the moment when a person realizes they have an idea that could solve a problem or fulfill a need. The ideation stage involves brainstorming, research, and validation. Successful entrepreneurs know how to validate their ideas and identify if it has the potential to become a successful business.

After the ideation stage comes the planning stage. It's when entrepreneurs create a roadmap for their business. It includes defining the target market, developing a business model, and crafting a brand. During this stage, entrepreneurs also learn how to overcome the fear of failure, which can be a significant obstacle for many entrepreneurs.

The next stage is the launch stage. It's when the entrepreneur officially starts their business. It's an exciting and daunting stage, as it requires entrepreneurs to take risks and make tough decisions. Launching a business requires resilience, persistence, and patience.

Once the business is up and running, entrepreneurs enter the growth stage. It's when the focus is on expanding their business, increasing profits, and developing their team. Entrepreneurs need to stay flexible during this stage, as growth can be unpredictable.

Finally, the last stage is the maturity stage. It's when the business has reached its goals, and entrepreneurs need to maintain and sustain their business's success. It requires a focus on innovation, continuous learning, and strategic planning to ensure long-term success.

Understanding the journey of an entrepreneur is critical to developing an entrepreneurial mindset. It helps entrepreneurs anticipate obstacles, adapt to change, and stay resilient during tough times. A successful entrepreneur sees each stage of the journey as an opportunity to learn and grow, to become a better entrepreneur, and make a more significant impact on the world.

Stages of Entrepreneurship

Starting a business is a journey with various stages, and the success of your business will depend on how you navigate those stages. Therefore, it's important to understand the different stages of entrepreneurship, so you can prepare accordingly.

Idea Generation: This is the first stage of entrepreneurship, where you generate an idea for a product or service. This idea can be born out of personal experience, market research, or a combination of both. The key is to identify a problem and create a solution that will satisfy a need in the market.

Feasibility Analysis: Once you have an idea, you need to determine if it's feasible. This involves researching your target market, analyzing your competition, and evaluating the financial viability of your idea. A comprehensive feasibility analysis can help you determine if your idea is worth pursuing or if you need to go back to the drawing board.

Business Planning: If your idea passes the feasibility analysis, then it's time to create a business plan. A well-developed business plan will provide a roadmap for your business and help you secure funding. It should include a summary of your business, market analysis, marketing and sales strategies, financial projections, and an executive summary.

Launch: Once your business plan is complete, it's time to launch your business. This involves setting up your business infrastructure, creating your products or services, and getting them to market. It's essential to carefully manage your resources during this stage and prioritize your goals to ensure a successful launch.

Growth and Scalability: After successfully launching your business, the next stage is to grow and scale. This involves developing a sales and marketing strategy to increase revenue, building a team to support growth, and improving operational efficiency. Growth can be challenging, and it requires careful planning and execution to avoid common pitfalls.

Maturity: The final stage of entrepreneurship is maturity, where your business has stabilized, and operations have become routine. At this stage, it's essential to maintain your competitive edge and continue to innovate to stay relevant in your market. Maturity can also present new opportunities for growth through expansion, strategic partnerships, or diversification.

The journey of an entrepreneur is filled with various stages, and the success of your business depends on how well you navigate those stages. Understanding the stages of entrepreneurship can help you prepare for the challenges and opportunities that lie ahead, and increase your chances of success.

Challenges and Opportunities at Each Stage

Starting your own business can be a challenging and rewarding journey. Understanding the challenges and opportunities at each stage is crucial to maintaining momentum and growing your business.

The first stage is the ideation stage. This is when you come up with a business idea and start to validate it. There are many challenges and opportunities at this stage. For example, you may struggle to successfully validate your idea, but you also have the freedom to be creative and explore different possibilities.

The second stage is the start-up stage. At this point, you have validated your idea and are ready to start building your business. This stage comes with its own set of challenges and opportunities. You may struggle with securing funding, but you also have the opportunity to build a strong team and establish a foundation for your business.

The third stage is the growth stage. This is when your business starts to take off and gain momentum. At this stage, you may face challenges with managing rapid growth, but you also have the opportunity to scale your business and reach a larger audience.

The final stage is the maturity stage. At this point, your business has established itself and is generating consistent revenue. The challenges at this stage include remaining relevant in a constantly changing market, but you also have the opportunity to innovate and expand your business in new ways.

The journey of an entrepreneur is full of both challenges and opportunities. Understanding what to expect at each stage can help you navigate the ups and downs of starting and growing a successful business.

How to Navigate the Entrepreneurial Journey

Embarking on the path of entrepreneurship is a unique journey that is challenging and rewarding. It is a path that requires a lot of determination, hard work, and sacrifice. The entrepreneurial journey can be full of ups and downs, and it is essential to understand the process and how to navigate it effectively.

The first step in navigating the entrepreneurial journey is to understand that it is not a straight line. It is a journey full of twist and turns, and it requires constant adaptation to new situations. The journey is not just about starting and running a business; it's about personal growth and development as well.

To navigate the entrepreneurial journey, it is essential to have a clear understanding of your goals and vision. You should have a clear idea of what you want to achieve and why you want to achieve it. Your goals should be specific, measurable, achievable, relevant, and time-bound. Having clear goals will help you stay focused and motivated throughout the journey.

Another important aspect of navigating the entrepreneurial journey is to embrace failure. Failure is not something to fear, but rather an opportunity to learn and grow. The most successful entrepreneurs have experienced failure and have learned from their mistakes. Embracing failure and learning from it will keep you on the path to success.

It is also essential to have a support system in place. Entrepreneurship can be a lonely journey, and having people who believe in you and your vision can make all the difference. Your support system can be family, friends, mentors, or a community of like-minded entrepreneurs. They can offer advice, encouragement, and support when you need it most.

Finally, navigating the entrepreneurial journey requires continuous learning and self-improvement. It is crucial to stay up to date with industry trends and best practices. Attend conferences, read books and blogs, and take courses to improve your skills and knowledge. By continuously improving yourself, you will be better equipped to handle challenges and capitalize on new opportunities.

Navigating the entrepreneurial journey requires a clear

understanding of your goals, embracing failure, having a support system in place and continuous learning and self-improvement. The journey may be challenging, but with the right mindset and approach, you can overcome obstacles and achieve success.

Importance of Perseverance and Resilience in Entrepreneurship

Every entrepreneur's journey is unique; however, one trait that all successful entrepreneurs share is their perseverance and resilience. Starting and running a business could be a roller coaster ride, where you have to deal with unexpected challenges, failures, and setbacks. That is why having resilience and perseverance is crucial to succeed in entrepreneurship.

Perseverance is the determination to keep pushing forward, no matter what happens. The road to success is paved with failures, rejections, and setbacks, and those who persevere will eventually overcome them. Resilience is the ability to adapt to changing circumstances and bounce back from failures and setbacks. Resilient entrepreneurs take the lessons they learn from their failures and use them to improve and grow.

One of the reasons why perseverance and resilience are essential in entrepreneurship is that it takes time to build a successful business. It requires hard work, commitment, and patience. It's easy to become discouraged when things don't go according to plan, but entrepreneurs who persevere and have resilience continue to pursue their goals, regardless of how many obstacles they face.

Furthermore, perseverance and resilience are necessary when it comes to making difficult decisions. Entrepreneurs must make tough choices regularly, often with limited information or time. Resilient entrepreneurs can take a step back and assess the situation from different angles before making an informed decision. Additionally, they are not afraid to admit when they've made a mistake and adapt their approach.

Perseverance and resilience are traits that every entrepreneur should have when starting and running a business. Entrepreneurs who possess these qualities can overcome challenges, adapt to change, and stay focused on their goals, ultimately achieving success in their chosen field.

Understanding Your Strengths and Weaknesses

Identifying Your Strengths

The Importance of Identifying Your Strengths

In order to embrace the entrepreneurial mindset, it is essential to understand your own unique strengths and weaknesses. Strengths are positive qualities and characteristics that come naturally to you and give you a sense of accomplishment and fulfillment. They are the skills and abilities that set you apart from others and make you a valuable contributor.

Identifying your strengths is essential because it allows you to focus on what you do best, and build a career or business around those strengths. By leveraging your strengths, you can build a competitive advantage and excel in your chosen field.

Furthermore, identifying your strengths can help you gain a better understanding of your personal values, goals and aspirations. This self-awareness can help you chart a clear path towards success and enable you to make better decisions about your career or business.

In this section, we will discuss the importance of identifying your strengths, and explore some effective techniques for discovering what you do best. By the end of this section, you will be equipped with the knowledge and tools you need to identify and leverage your strengths, and take your business or career to the next level.

Techniques for Identifying Your Strengths

As you begin to embark on your own entrepreneurial journey, it's important to have a clear understanding of your personal strengths. These are the skills and abilities that come naturally to you, the things that you excel at without much effort. When you have a solid understanding of your strengths, you can leverage them to your advantage, using them to build a business that plays to your unique talents.

But how do you go about identifying your strengths? Here are a few techniques that may help:

Ask for feedback: Reach out to friends, colleagues, and trusted advisors and ask them to provide honest feedback about your strengths. Sometimes, it can be difficult to see our own strengths clearly, but others may have a more objective perspective.

Take personality tests: There are a variety of personality tests available that can help you identify your unique strengths and traits. Consider taking tests such as the Myers-Briggs Type Indicator or the StrengthsFinder assessment.

Look to past successes: Consider the things you've accomplished in your life so far. What were you doing when you were at your best? What tasks or projects have you undertaken that came most naturally to you?

Keep a journal: Take a few minutes each day to jot down your thoughts and feelings about your work. Note the tasks that energized you and the ones that drained you. Over time, you may begin to see patterns emerge that can help you identify your strengths.

Your strengths are what make you unique, and they are ultimately what will set you apart as an entrepreneur. By taking the time to identify and understand them, you can build a business that plays to your strengths and allows you to truly thrive.

Assessing Your Strengths Regularly

As an entrepreneur, it is crucial to be aware of your strengths to make the most out of them. You must assess your abilities regularly to fine-tune your strengths and develop them further. Many successful entrepreneurs share the same trait; they regularly take stock of their skills and knowledge to improve them.

Assessing your strengths regularly involves taking a closer look at a few key areas. Firstly, you need to identify any activities that come naturally and effortlessly to you. These activities could be skills such as communication skills, leadership skills, or technical skills. Additionally, consider the tasks that you enjoy doing and those that give you a sense of accomplishment.

Another important aspect of identifying your strengths is to look for activities that you are consistently performing well. Observe your past successes and try to understand the factors that contributed to them. Think about the feedback you've received from others on your work and consider areas where you have been praised.

Once you have identified your strengths, it's essential to leverage them in your personal and professional pursuits. You can use your strengths to improve your weaknesses, delegate tasks that are not your strong points, or enhance your overall effectiveness.

Finally, remember that identifying your strengths is not a one-time task. Regularly reflecting on your abilities can help you stay up to date with your ever-evolving strengths and adjust your strategic priorities accordingly. By doing so, you can continually develop yourself as an entrepreneur, ultimately leading to greater success.

Overcoming Fear of Acknowledging Your Strengths

Confidence in oneself is one of the critical factors that aid success in entrepreneurship. However, many people fail to take the first step towards finding their strengths and leveraging them because of the fear of acknowledging their strengths. This fear could stem from the belief that acknowledging strengths may come across as arrogance or lead to complacency.

But, in reality, acknowledging strengths is a powerful tool that can unlock potential and fuel progress. To overcome the fear of acknowledging strengths, one must start by understanding that strengths aren't just about being 'good at something'. A strength is a combination of skills, experiences, and knowledge that allows an individual to perform better than an average in a particular area.

When one acknowledges their strengths, they become aware of their potential, which allows them to find ways to fulfill it. Additionally, accepting strengths allows individuals to identify what motivates them and what activities should be prioritized. With this realization, it's possible to focus on activities that align with what an individual enjoys doing and what they excel at, leading to positive results.

Acknowledging strengths also allows one to develop self-awareness, which is crucial in entrepreneurship. In self-awareness, entrepreneurs learn their working style, communication methods, and decision-making processes, increasing the likelihood of success in the long term.

Ultimately, there's no harm in acknowledging one's strengths. In fact, it's a powerful tool for self-awareness and self-advancement in the entrepreneurial journey.

Maximizing Your Strengths to Overcome Weaknesses

Identifying your strengths and weaknesses is an important part of developing an entrepreneurial mindset. Once you understand where your strengths lie, you'll be able to focus on leveraging them to overcome your weaknesses.

To start, take some time to think about your natural abilities and what you're good at. Write down a list of your strengths, whether they're hard skills like coding or graphic design, or soft skills like communication or problem-solving.

Once you have a solid list of your strengths, think about how you can use them to overcome your weaknesses. For example, if you struggle with public speaking, but you're great at creating visual presentations, you can focus on putting together a dynamic and engaging slide deck to support your speaking.

Another way to maximize your strengths is to build a team around you that complements your skills. If you're not great at managing finances, but you have a team member who is, you can rely on them to help you navigate that part of your business.

Remember that your strengths and weaknesses can change over time as you learn and grow. Keep revisiting your list and adjusting it as necessary, and continually seek out ways to leverage your strengths to become a more effective entrepreneur.

Acknowledging Your Weaknesses

The Importance of Acknowledging Your Weaknesses

In order to become a successful entrepreneur, it is imperative to have a clear understanding of your strengths and weaknesses. While acknowledging your strengths might seem like a more comfortable task, addressing weaknesses can be more challenging, as it requires a level of vulnerability and self-awareness that many people find difficult to confront. However, failing to acknowledge and address one's weaknesses can lead to significant setbacks in business growth and development.

Acknowledging one's weaknesses is particularly important as it provides an opportunity for personal and professional growth. When entrepreneurs are aware of their weaknesses, they can position themselves to either develop and improve in areas where they are lacking or leverage the strengths of others to fill those gaps. This not only helps to mitigate risks but also strengthens the overall team and increases the likelihood of success.

Moreover, acknowledging one's weaknesses promotes transparency and honesty in business dealings. As an entrepreneur, being open about areas where you struggle can give investors, stakeholders, partners, and employees more confidence in your leadership abilities. It demonstrates that you have a realistic view of yourself and your business, and are willing to set aside your ego in order to better serve your team and customers.

While it may be uncomfortable to acknowledge one's

limitations, it is crucial for entrepreneurs to do so in order to promote growth, strengthen their team, and foster trust within their business community.

Techniques for Acknowledging Your Weaknesses

Acknowledging your weaknesses is not always easy. It requires a certain level of humility and the willingness to accept constructive feedback. Here are some techniques for acknowledging your weaknesses:

Seek feedback: One of the best ways to identify your weaknesses is by asking others for feedback. This can be done through formal performance reviews or by simply asking for input from colleagues, friends, or family members. It's important to approach this with an open mind and a willingness to listen to constructive feedback.

Conduct a self-assessment: Another way to identify weaknesses is to conduct a self-assessment. This involves taking an honest look at your skills, knowledge, and experience to identify areas where you may need improvement. This can be done through journaling or reflecting on your past experiences.

Use objective assessments: There are several objective assessments that can help you identify your weaknesses, such as Myers-Briggs Type Indicator (MBTI), StrengthsFinder, or Emotional Intelligence (EI) assessments. These assessments are designed to provide insight into your personality traits, strengths, and weaknesses.

Focus on continuous learning: Acknowledging your

weaknesses is just the first step. It's important to take action to improve upon them. This can be done through continuous learning, such as attending workshops, taking courses, or reading books on the subject. It's important to have a growth mindset and embrace challenges as opportunities to learn and grow.

By acknowledging your weaknesses and taking action to improve upon them, you can develop a strong sense of self-awareness and become a more effective business owner.

Identifying Areas for Improvement

In order to become a successful entrepreneur, it's important to acknowledge your weaknesses and work on improving them. This can be a difficult task, as it requires a level of self-awareness and honesty about your capabilities. However, by recognizing your weaknesses, you can make a plan to address them and better position yourself for success.

The first step in identifying areas for improvement is to assess your skills and experiences objectively. Consider the areas where you have struggled in the past, or where you feel less confident. Take note of any feedback you have received from others, both positive and negative, as well as any failures or setbacks you have experienced.

It's important to approach this process without judgment or self-criticism. Remember that everyone has weaknesses, and it's a natural part of the learning process. By embracing this mindset, you can approach your weaknesses with a sense of curiosity and a willingness to learn and grow.

Once you have identified areas for improvement, create a plan to address them. This may involve seeking out new experiences or opportunities, taking on projects that challenge you, or seeking out feedback and mentorship from others.

Remember that improvement takes time and effort, but by acknowledging your weaknesses and working to improve them, you can become a stronger, more versatile entrepreneur.

Overcoming Fear of Acknowledging Your Weaknesses

Acknowledging weaknesses is never easy. But, as an entrepreneur, it is essential to accept that you cannot do everything on your own. The key to overcoming the fear of acknowledging your weaknesses is to change your perception of weakness. Weaknesses should not be viewed as a hindrance but as an opportunity to improve and grow.

One of the main reasons people fear acknowledging their weaknesses is the fear of being judged or ridiculed. It is crucial to understand that everyone has weaknesses, even the most successful entrepreneurs. Acknowledging your weaknesses shows that you're self-aware and willing to learn.

Another way to overcome the fear of acknowledging your weaknesses is to focus on the positive outcomes that come with it. When you acknowledge your weaknesses, you can work on improving them and, in turn, become a better entrepreneur. Your strengths can help you succeed, but your weaknesses can also hold you back. Acknowledging and improving your weaknesses can unlock new opportunities for growth and success.

Lastly, it is essential to remember that acknowledging your weaknesses is not a sign of failure. Failure is not acknowledging your weaknesses and refusing to work on them. Successful entrepreneurs are not afraid of exposing their vulnerabilities because they understand that growth and success come from continuous learning and improvement.

Overcoming the fear of acknowledging your weaknesses is vital to becoming a successful entrepreneur. Changing your perception of weakness, focusing on the positive outcomes, and understanding that it is not a sign of failure are key steps to take to overcome this fear. Remember that weaknesses are an opportunity for growth and improvement, and accepting them can unlock new opportunities for success.

Seeking Help and Support to Overcome Weaknesses

No one is perfect, and every entrepreneur has weaknesses that are holding them back. Fortunately, you don't have to overcome these weaknesses alone. Seeking out help and support can be a powerful way to overcome your weaknesses and achieve success.

One of the best ways to get help with your weaknesses is to work with a mentor or coach. A mentor can help you identify your weaknesses, provide you with the tools you need to overcome them, and offer you feedback and guidance as you work to improve.

Another option is to work with a business partner who has a different set of skills than you do. This can help balance out your strengths and weaknesses and make your business more effective as a whole.

You can also seek out support from family and friends. Having people in your life who believe in you and support your goals can be incredibly valuable when it comes to overcoming your weaknesses.

Finally, don't be afraid to seek out professional help when you need it. Whether you need help with your finances, your marketing strategy, or your leadership skills, there are professionals out there who can provide you with the assistance you need to succeed.

Leveraging Strengths to Overcome Weaknesses

Understanding the Relationship Between Strengths and Weaknesses

As you become familiar with your strengths and weaknesses, you'll start to notice that the two are often related. For example, you might be a great public speaker but struggle with organization and planning. By leveraging your strength in public speaking, you can overcome your weakness in planning by participating in more speaking engagements, which forces you to plan and organize your speeches well.

Likewise, if you're an expert in a specific area but lack experience in another, you can leverage your strengths to gain more knowledge and experience. Collaborating with someone who has the skills you need or taking courses to develop another area of expertise can help you address your weaknesses.

It's also important to note that your strengths and weaknesses may change over time. As you gain more experience and knowledge, what once was a weakness may become a strength. So it's essential to reassess your strengths and weaknesses regularly and adjust your strategy accordingly.

Finally, remember that it's not about being perfect or having no weaknesses. All successful entrepreneurs have areas of weakness, but what sets them apart is their ability to leverage their strengths, continuously improve, and surround themselves with a strong team to overcome any challenges.

Identifying Opportunities to Leverage Your Strengths

One critical aspect of leveraging your strengths is identifying opportunities where they can be utilized to overcome your weaknesses. By understanding your strengths and weaknesses, you can pinpoint areas where your strengths can offset your weaknesses, leading to more effective decision-making and problem-solving.

For example, if your weakness is in sales and marketing, but your strength is in product development, you can leverage your product development skills to create a product that is so good it practically sells itself, eliminating the need for high-pressure sales tactics. Alternatively, you could leverage your product development skills to create a product that is highly differentiated from the competition, making marketing easier and paving the way for higher sales.

Another example is if you struggle with time management, but you excel at delegating tasks and managing others. You can leverage this to delegate tasks to others who are better suited for them, freeing up your time to focus on strategic planning and other high-level tasks.

It's worth noting that leveraging your strengths doesn't mean ignoring your weaknesses altogether. Instead, it means finding creative ways to work around or compensate for them. By doing this, you can focus on what you're good at while still addressing areas that need improvement.

Techniques for Developing Your Weaknesses

Everyone has their weaknesses. Identifying your weaknesses in a particular area is the first step towards developing stronger skills. However, it is not enough to just recognize and acknowledge your weaknesses. You need to work towards improving in those areas. Here are some techniques you can use to develop your weaknesses:

Seek feedback - Understanding how others perceive you can help you identify areas where you need improvement. Seek feedback from colleagues, friends, family, mentors, or coaches who you trust to give you honest feedback.

Set achievable goals - Once you have identified your weaknesses, set goals that will help you work on your areas of weakness. Break the goals into smaller, achievable steps that can be easily tracked and monitored.

Focus on improving one area at a time - It may be tempting to try and fix all your weaknesses at the same time. However, this approach can be overwhelming and lead to burnout. Instead, focus on improving one area at a time and then move on to the next.

Learn from others - Look for people who excel in the areas where you are weak and learn from them. This could be through reading their books, attending their workshops or seminars, or even working with them one on one as a mentor or coach.

Practice, practice, practice - The more you practice, the better you become. Look for opportunities to practice your weak skills. It could be through volunteering, taking on new challenges at work, or even starting a side project.

By leveraging your strengths to overcome your weaknesses, you can become a more well-rounded and effective entrepreneur. Remember, no one is perfect, but by consistently working on your weaknesses, you can continue to grow and develop both personally and professionally.

Embracing a Growth Mindset to Overcome Weaknesses

As an entrepreneur, it is inevitable that you will have weaknesses. Nobody can excel at everything, and it's important to recognize and acknowledge where you struggle. However, just because you have weaknesses doesn't mean you can't overcome them. In fact, one of the key tenets of the entrepreneurial mindset is embracing a growth mindset, allowing you to persevere through challenges and develop new skills and strengths.

The first step in leveraging your strengths to overcome weakness is to identify what areas you struggle with the most. This could be anything from public speaking to financial management to time management. Once you have pinpointed your weaknesses, it's time to start thinking about how you can develop new skills and strengthen your existing ones.

One effective way to do this is by adopting a growth mindset. This means embracing the idea that your abilities and intelligence are not fixed, but can be developed through hard work and dedication. When you approach challenges with a growth mindset, you are more likely to push yourself out of your comfort zone and try new things. You may make mistakes along the way, but you will learn from them and become stronger as a result.

Another way to leverage your strengths is to partner with people who have complementary skills. For example, if you struggle with finance, you may want to team up with someone who excels in that area. By working together, you can leverage each other's strengths and compensate for each other's weaknesses.

Finally, it's important to recognize that success is not only about overcoming weaknesses, but also about capitalizing on your strengths. When you focus on what you're good at, you can build a business that plays to your strengths and sets you up for long-term success.

By embracing a growth mindset, partnering with complementary skills, and focusing on your strengths, you can leverage your abilities to overcome weaknesses and achieve your entrepreneurial goals.

Evaluating Your Progress and Adjusting Your Strategies

Once you have leveraged your strengths to overcome your weaknesses, it's important to continually evaluate your progress and adjust your strategies accordingly. The entrepreneurial journey is not a straight line, and adjustments will need to be made along the way.

One effective strategy for evaluating progress is to set realistic and measurable goals. These goals should be based on your strengths, weaknesses, and overall vision for your business. By regularly tracking your progress towards these goals, you can identify areas where you are excelling and areas where you need to improve.

Once you have identified areas where you need to improve, it's time to adjust your strategies. This might mean seeking out a mentor or business coach who can offer guidance and help you develop new skills. It might also mean pivoting your business strategy, refining your product or service offerings, or revisiting your target audience.

It's important to remember that leveraging your strengths to overcome weaknesses is an ongoing process. As your business grows and evolves, you will face new challenges and opportunities. By continually evaluating your progress and adjusting your strategies, you can ensure that you are always moving forward towards your vision for success.

Creating a Vision for Your Business

Understanding the Importance of a Clear Vision

Aligning Your Goals and Values

When an entrepreneur sets out to create a vision for their business, the first step is to get clear on their goals and values. This is an important indicator of what the business represents to them, and what they want it to achieve. For some, the goal may be to create a sustainable source of income that supports their family, while for others, it may be to make a significant impact on a particular industry.

Before creating a vision, it's important to do an exercise in introspection. This helps determine the things that truly matter to the entrepreneur when it comes to their business. Some questions to consider include:

- What motivates me to start this business?
- What are my core values?
- What is important to me beyond financial gains?
- What is the mission statement for my business?

If a person's values and goals are not aligned with the vision for their business, they will likely experience a disconnect between their personal aspirations and their business objectives. This could lead to burnout, frustration or even failure.

Once the personal goals and values have been identified, it's time to craft a vision for the business. A clear business vision can inspire employees, prospects, and stakeholders, leading to greater success. The vision of the business should resonate with the values and objectives of the entrepreneur.

Create a vision statement that is inspiring and purposeful, using language that reflects the entrepreneur's core values. Keep the vision statement concise and memorable so that employees, customers, and partners can easily communicate it to others.

Once the vision for the business has been determined, the next step is to map out the specific steps required to achieve that vision. The importance of creating a clear vision for a business cannot be overstated, as it serves as a guiding light for all other business-related decisions.

Developing a Big Picture View

Before you even begin to create a business plan, you need to develop a clear and concise vision for your business. This can be difficult, but it's crucial for your success. One of the initial steps for creating a vision is to develop a big picture view. Essentially, you need to take a step back and look at things from a broad perspective.

What does this mean? It means considering the overarching goals of your business - why are you starting it in the first place? What are you trying to achieve? Where do you see the business in the next five or ten years? Answering these questions will give you a better understanding of the ultimate objective of your venture.

Having a big picture view of your business will help you stay focused and motivated when things get difficult. When you have a clear understanding of what you're working towards, it'll be easier to make decisions that align with those goals. Additionally, having a clear vision will help you communicate your goals with your team and stakeholders. It'll help them understand why they're working with you and how they can contribute to the overall success of the company.

Developing a big picture view is an important step in creating a clear and concise vision for your business. It'll help you focus on what's most important and give you a roadmap for achieving success.

Setting a Clear Direction

As an entrepreneur, having a clear direction is crucial to the success of your business. Without a clear sense of where you are going or what you want to achieve, it can be challenging to make strategic decisions and move forward. Setting a clear direction begins with understanding the core values and purpose behind your business.

To identify your core values, start by asking yourself what motivates you to be an entrepreneur. What are your beliefs and how do you want to make a difference in the world? Once you've answered these questions, consider the values that are essential to your business. These could be anything from honesty and integrity to creativity and innovation. Write down your core values and keep them in mind as you move forward.

Next, identify your business's purpose. This is your company's reason for existence, beyond just making a profit. What problem does your business solve or what need does it fulfill? Defining your purpose will help you stay focused on what really matters and guide decision-making in the future.

Finally, set a clear direction by defining your long-term vision. This is a statement of where you see your business going in the next 3-5 years. Your vision should inspire and motivate you and your team, providing a sense of direction for everything you do.

By setting a clear direction for your business, you are laying the foundation for future success. Your core values, purpose, and long-term vision provide the framework for decision-making and help you stay focused on what really matters.

Communicating Your Vision

A clear vision is essential for any business to succeed. Once you have established the vision for your business, it is essential to communicate it effectively to your team, stakeholders, and customers. Effective communication of your vision will help ensure everyone is on the same page and working towards the same goals.

The first step in communicating your vision is to identify your target audience. The way you communicate your vision will vary depending on who you are speaking to. For example, you may need to use different language when speaking to potential investors versus speaking to your team members.

Once you have identified your target audience, it is time to craft your message. Start by focusing on the why behind your vision. Help your audience understand the problem you are trying to solve and the impact you hope to make.

Next, focus on the how. Explain the steps you plan to take to make your vision a reality. This may include outlining your business strategy, talking about your team, and sharing your timeline.

Finally, wrap up your message with a call to action. What do you want your audience to do after hearing your message? Whether it's join your team, invest in your business, or become a customer, make sure you are clear about what you want.

Remember, communicating your vision is an ongoing process. It's not a one-time event. You will need to revisit your message regularly and make adjustments as your business grows and evolves.

Inspiring and Motivating Others

As an entrepreneur, it is essential to have a clear vision for your business. But, simply having a vision is not enough. To grow your business, you must be able to inspire and motivate others to invest in your vision. Your vision should be clear, concise, and compelling.

When your employees and customers understand your vision, they will be more likely to align their goals and actions with the direction of the business. This alignment will increase productivity, engagement, and loyalty.

To inspire and motivate others, you need to communicate your vision effectively. The way you communicate your vision should be simple, memorable, and easy to understand. Use stories, analogies, and metaphors to paint a vivid picture of your vision.

It is also essential to live and breathe your vision. As a leader, you should embody the values and principles that guide your business. Be authentic and transparent in your communication and actions.

Finally, empower and delegate to others. Your employees and partners are essential in realizing your vision. Give them the freedom and resources they need to succeed. When you believe in them and their abilities, they will believe in you and your vision.

Remember, your vision is not just a statement on a piece of paper. It is a way of life. When you understand the importance of a clear vision and can inspire and motivate others to believe in it, your business will grow and thrive.

Steps for Creating a Vision

Identifying Your Strengths and Weaknesses

When it comes to creating a vision for your business, it is crucial to first identify your own strengths and weaknesses. You need to have a clear understanding of what you are good at and what you struggle with, so you can build a team around you that complements your strengths and compensates for your weaknesses.

To identify your strengths, start by taking an honest look at yourself. What do you excel at? What do others often praise you for? What activities and tasks do you enjoy doing? You can also reflect on past successes and accomplishments to gain insights into where you shine.

On the other hand, identifying weaknesses can often be more challenging. It can be uncomfortable to admit what you are not good at or where you struggle. However, it is essential to be honest with yourself to avoid potential pitfalls down the road. You can ask yourself questions such as: What tasks do I avoid or procrastinate on? What areas have I received negative feedback or struggled with in the past? What skills do I lack that could be important for my business?

Once you have a clear understanding of your strengths and weaknesses, you can start to think about how to surround yourself with the right people to build a successful business. This could mean hiring employees or contractors who complement your skill set or partnering with other businesses or entrepreneurs who bring different strengths to the table.

Remember, having a clear understanding of your strengths and weaknesses is just the beginning of creating a successful business vision. It takes time, effort, and a willingness to adapt and evolve as your business grows and changes.

Assessing Your Market and Industry

After developing a clear understanding of the importance of a vision for your business in the previous section, it is time to start creating one. Creating a vision requires a comprehensive understanding of your industry and target market. After all, your vision should be based on feasible market demands, existing gaps, and areas for innovation.

Assessing your market should start with identifying your target customer. Create detailed profiles of your target customers, including demographic information, their pain points, and how your product or service can solve their problems. Once you have identified your target market, you need to analyze the market trends, competitors, and consumer behavior.

Market trends can reveal growth potential or primary drivers for change, such as new technologies or emerging threats. Analyzing your competitors' strategies and identifying their strengths and weaknesses can provide valuable insights for creating your vision. Understanding your consumers' behavior increases your chances of developing a vision that resonates with them.

After the initial assessment, it's time to gather data through surveys, interviews, and focus groups. Feedback from consumers can lead to valuable insights and help refine your vision. Understand their purchasing habits, preferences and what drives them to buy similar products.

Assessing your market and industry is crucial for creating a vision that is based on realistic expectations and meaningful goals. The process is complex and requires constant monitoring and adaptation to changes in the market, but it's a necessary step that can determine the success of your business.

Defining Your Target Audience

As an entrepreneur, it's critical to have a clear vision for your business. This vision should be well-defined, realistic, and one that you're passionate about, as it'll serve as a blueprint for achieving your goals. One key aspect of crafting a great vision is defining your target audience.

Your target audience is the group of individuals or businesses that are most likely to benefit from what you have to offer. Understanding them is crucial as it'll make it easier to develop and market your products or services to them effectively. Here are some steps on how to define your target audience:

First, conduct market research to identify your potential customers' demographics, interests, preferences, and behaviors. This information will help you understand your target audience's behavior and pain points, which you can address in your products or services. Analyze data such as age, gender, location, education level, income, spending patterns, etc.

Second, create personas that represent your target audience. A persona is a fictional character that reflects a particular group of prospects you want to reach. It helps you understand the needs, values, and preferences of your customers better. Build your personas based on the research you conducted, and give them a name, job title, and even a photo.

Third, segment your target audience based on common characteristics they share. This allows you to customize your marketing messages and offerings for each group. You might segment your audience based on things like age, gender, occupation, location, interests, etc.

Fourth, analyze the competition within your market niche. Identify what they're doing well and where they're falling short, and then find ways to differentiate yourself. This process will help you create a unique selling proposition (USP) for your business, which is vital to attracting and retaining customers.

By understanding your target audience, you can create a compelling vision that aligns with their needs and helps them achieve their goals. It'll also ensure your business is on track to success as you have a clear understanding of who you are serving and how you can serve them better.

Establishing Long-term and Short-term Goals

When starting any venture, it's important to have a vision that can guide you through both the good times and the bad. This vision is the framework for everything you will do in your business, so it's worth taking the time to get it right.

To create a vision for your business, you need to establish both long-term and short-term goals. Long-term goals are the big-picture objectives that you want to achieve in the future. These goals may be aspirational, such as becoming a leader in your industry or expanding to international markets. Or they may be more focused on financial performance or market share. Whatever your long-term goals, it's important to have a clear picture of where you want your business to be in the years to come.

Short-term goals, on the other hand, are the smaller steps that you'll take to reach your long-term objectives. They are the building blocks that will help you achieve incremental progress towards your vision. Short-term goals might include things like launching a new product, increasing your social media following, or improving your customer retention rate. By breaking your vision down into specific short-term goals, you can create a roadmap for achieving your long-term objectives.

When creating your goals, it's important to make sure that they are both realistic and ambitious. You want your goals to be achievable, but you also want them to push you outside of your comfort zone. This balance is essential for staying motivated and making meaningful progress towards your vision.

In addition to setting goals, it's also important to establish a timeline for achieving them. This will help you stay accountable and measure your progress along the way. Consider breaking your goals down into quarterly or yearly targets, and track your progress towards these milestones over time. This will help you stay focused and motivated, even when things get tough.

Finally, it's important to communicate your vision and

goals clearly to your team. Your team should be aligned around your vision, and everyone should understand their role in achieving your goals. By creating a shared understanding of what you're trying to achieve, you can build a culture of collaboration and accountability that will be essential for achieving your vision.

Incorporating Flexibility into Your Vision

In creating a vision for your business, it's important to keep in mind that sometimes, things don't go as planned. That's why it's crucial to incorporate flexibility into your vision.

Flexibility allows you to adapt to changing situations and market conditions. It means that you're open to new ideas and that you're willing to pivot when necessary. While having a clear vision is important, being flexible ensures that you're able to stay on course, even when things get tough.

Incorporating flexibility into your vision requires you to:

Be willing to change course: While it's important to have a clear direction, you must also be willing to change your mind. Flexibility means that you're open to new ideas and can adapt to changing circumstances.

Keep an open mind: Be willing to listen to feedback and to consider new ways of doing things. A closed mind is not conducive to growth and can limit your ability to make the most of opportunities.

Stay focused on your goals: Being flexible doesn't mean that you should abandon your goals altogether. It simply means that you should be willing to adjust your approach in order to achieve them.

Create a plan B: Even the best-laid plans can go awry. That's why it's important to have a backup plan in place. Be prepared to pivot if necessary, and have contingencies in place to deal with unexpected situations.

Incorporating flexibility into your vision can help you weather any storms that come your way. It allows you to stay agile and responsive, giving you the best chance of success in the long run.

Turning Your Vision into Reality

Taking Action towards Your Goals

When it comes to turning your vision into reality, taking action towards your goals becomes crucial. It's important to remember that your vision is only as good as your ability to make it a reality. Here are some steps to help you take action towards your goals:

Set specific, measurable, and achievable goals: In order to take action towards your vision, you need to set specific, measurable, and achievable goals. This will help you break down your vision into manageable steps and stay focused on what you want to achieve.

Define your strategy: Once you have set your goals, it's important to define your strategy. This includes identifying the resources you need, creating a timeline, and determining the actions you need to take.

Take small steps: Taking action towards your goals can be overwhelming, which is why it's important to take small steps. Break down your strategy into small, actionable tasks that you can complete each day. Celebrate each milestone you achieve.

Stay focused on your goals: Distractions can be a major obstacle when it comes to taking action towards your goals. Stay focused on your goals by avoiding distractions, setting priorities, and learning to say "no" when necessary.

Measure your progress: Regularly measuring your progress towards your goals will help you stay on track and make any necessary adjustments to your strategy. Celebrate your successes and use your setbacks as learning opportunities.

Remember, turning your vision into reality requires commitment, perseverance, and the ability to take action towards your goals. By setting specific, measurable, and achievable goals, defining your strategy, taking small steps, staying focused, and measuring your progress, you can make your vision a reality.

Measuring and Tracking Progress

Once you have a clear vision for your business, it's essential to measure and track your progress towards achieving that vision. Without measuring progress, it's difficult to know if you're on the right track and if you're making progress towards your goals.

There are several ways to measure progress, and it's important to identify the most effective methods for your business. Here are some steps to help you measure and track your progress towards achieving your vision:

Identify Key Performance Indicators (KPIs)

It's crucial to determine the KPIs that indicate progress towards achieving your vision. These KPIs can include financial metrics such as revenue, profit, and cash flow, as well as non-financial metrics such as customer satisfaction, employee engagement, and market share.

Set Targets

Once you have identified your KPIs, set targets for each of

them. These targets should be specific, measurable, achievable, relevant, and time-bound.

Monitor Progress

Regularly monitor and measure your progress towards achieving your targets. This can be done weekly, monthly, quarterly, or annually, depending on the KPIs and targets.

Analyze Results

Once you have measured your progress, analyze the results to identify areas where you're doing well and areas where you need improvement. Use this analysis to make informed decisions and adjust your strategy as necessary.

Take Action

Based on your analysis, take action to address any areas where you need improvement. This could involve implementing new processes or procedures, increasing marketing efforts, or making changes to your products or services.

Repeat the Process

Measuring and tracking progress is an ongoing process. Continually revisit your KPIs, targets, and progress to ensure you're on track towards achieving your vision. By regularly measuring and tracking progress, you can ensure you're making progress towards your goals and adjust your strategy as needed.

Making Adjustments and Refinements

Once you have set your vision and identified your goals, it's time to start executing your plan. However, it's important to keep in mind that your vision may not always be achievable or may need to be adjusted based on market trends or the needs of your customers. Making adjustments and refinements to your vision is a necessary part of the entrepreneurial journey that requires flexibility and adaptability.

One of the key factors in making adjustments to your vision is analyzing the data that you have collected. This includes data on your product or service, feedback from customers, and market trends. By analyzing this data, you can identify areas where your plan may need to be adjusted or refined to better align with your goals and customer needs.

Another important factor is having a growth mindset. This means being open to new ideas and perspectives, and embracing challenges as opportunities for growth. It's essential to understand that failure is a natural part of the process, and that making pivots and adjustments is necessary for success.

To make effective adjustments and refinements, it's important to have a clear understanding of your resources and capabilities. This includes understanding your team's skillsets, your budget, and your timeline. Assessing your resources allows you to make informed decisions about how to adjust your plan while still achieving your goals.

Finally, communication is key when making adjustments and refinements. This includes communicating with your team, stakeholders, and customers. Keeping everyone informed about changes and updates helps to build trust and ensures that everyone is aligned with your vision.

Making adjustments and refinements to your vision is a natural part of the entrepreneurial journey. By analyzing data, having a growth mindset, understanding your resources, and communicating effectively, you can make informed decisions that keep your business on track towards achieving your goals.

Staying Positive and Focused

Creating a Vision for Your Business
Once you have developed a clear vision for your business, it's time to focus on turning it into a reality. This is where many entrepreneurs falter because they get distracted, lose their focus, or simply give up. However, successful entrepreneurs know how to stay positive and focused on their vision, even during challenging times.

To stay positive and focused, it's important to have a growth mindset. This means believing that your talents and abilities can be developed through hard work and dedication. You must be willing to learn from your mistakes, embrace challenges as opportunities to grow, and persist in the face of setbacks.

Another way to stay positive and focused is to surround yourself with supportive people. Build a team of trusted advisors, mentors, and colleagues who believe in you and your vision. Seek out positive role models and learn from their experiences.

Finally, it's important to stay committed to your vision, even when it's difficult. This means setting goals, creating a plan of action, and tracking your progress. Celebrate your successes along the way and learn from your failures.

Remember, turning your vision into reality requires effort, dedication, and resilience. But with a positive mindset, a strong support system, and a clear plan of action, you can make your dreams a reality.

Celebrating Milestones and Achievements

As a business owner, it's essential to celebrate the successes and milestones of your journey. Celebrating these moments can help motivate you to keep pushing forward towards achieving your vision. It's important to take the time to recognize and enjoy the journey that you are on.

One way to celebrate your milestones is by taking a step back from your daily routine and reflecting on your progress. By acknowledging the progress that you have made, you can boost your confidence and momentum to keep moving forward.

Another great way to celebrate is by sharing your successes with others. Share your story on social media, create a blog post, or newsletter that highlights your accomplishments. Doing this not only acknowledges your hard work and dedication but also inspires others to follow in your footsteps.

Finally, you can celebrate your successes by rewarding yourself and your team. You can host a team dinner, plan a team outing, or offer incentives for those who have contributed to your accomplishments. Recognizing and rewarding the efforts of others is essential in cultivating a positive and productive work environment.

Celebrating milestones and achievements not only acknowledges your progress but also motivates and inspires you to keep working towards your vision. Taking the time to reflect and reward yourself and others is an essential part of creating a successful and fulfilling business.

Identifying and Analyzing Market Opportunities

Understanding Market Opportunities

What is a market opportunity?

Market opportunities are potential areas where a company can generate revenue and grow. Identifying market opportunities is a crucial aspect of the entrepreneurial mindset as it helps entrepreneurs determine which areas to focus on and how to structure their businesses.

A market opportunity can arise from a variety of factors such as changes in customer needs, advances in technology, or shifts in government regulations. Entrepreneurs must develop the ability to detect these changes and understand how they can be leveraged to create new businesses or expand existing ones.

To identify market opportunities, entrepreneurs must first identify their target customers, understand their needs, and determine what problems they are trying to solve. This information can be gathered through various methods including market research, surveys, or interviews with potential customers.

Once entrepreneurs have identified their target customer and their needs, they can begin to analyze the competitive landscape to understand what other solutions are available in the market. At this stage, entrepreneurs can identify gaps

71

in the market that they can fill with their products or services.

Another way to identify market opportunities is to observe trends in the industry or broader economy. Entrepreneurs must stay ahead of the curve and anticipate future demand for products and services. By identifying trends early, entrepreneurs can be better positioned to capitalize on emerging markets and new opportunities.

Identifying market opportunities is a continuous process that requires entrepreneurs to be constantly aware of changes in their industries and customer needs. Successful entrepreneurs are able to detect trends early and adapt their businesses accordingly to stay ahead of the competition.

The Importance of Recognizing Market Opportunities

As an entrepreneur, recognizing a market opportunity is crucial to the success of your business. The first step in identifying market opportunities is to have a broad understanding of what they are and why they matter.

Market opportunities are situations, trends, or needs that have the potential to become profitable business ventures. These opportunities arise due to changes in industries, technology, consumer behavior or gaps in the market. Entrepreneurs must remain vigilant and always on the lookout for unique opportunities that others may have missed.

Recognizing market opportunities is important for a couple of reasons. Firstly, it allows businesses to capitalize on new and emerging trends before they become mainstream. Secondly, it provides an avenue for growth and expansion beyond the original business model.

A good way to identify market opportunities is to ask questions about your industry and stay up-to-date with industry news and developments. Additionally, networking and talking to other entrepreneurs and thought leaders can help you understand the changing landscape of your industry.

By continuously analyzing the market and staying aware of trends, entrepreneurs can distinguish themselves by providing unique products or services that meet the changing needs of consumers. In a business world that is constantly evolving, the ability to identify and capitalize on market opportunities can mean the difference between success and failure.

Characteristics of a Good Market Opportunity

As you embark on your journey as an entrepreneur, identifying good market opportunities is critical to the survival of your business. Not every idea is a good one, and not every market is suited for your business. In this section, we'll discuss the characteristics of a good market opportunity so you can effectively evaluate your ideas and identify the most promising opportunities.

A good market opportunity is one that meets a specific need or solves a problem for a large group of people. It's important to think about the potential customers for your product or service and understand their behaviors and preferences. Additionally, a good market opportunity should have the potential for growth and sustainability over time.

Another characteristic of a good market opportunity is low competition or a unique differentiation from existing competition. You must find ways to differentiate yourself from competitors or create a new category altogether. This can be done through offering unique features, better pricing, superior customer service, or an innovative approach.

Lastly, a good market opportunity should align with your own interests and passions, as this will motivate you to work harder and stay committed to the idea. When you're passionate about a product or service, you're more likely to understand your target market and create a better product or service.

Identifying a good market opportunity is just the beginning. In the next sections, we'll discuss how to conduct market research and evaluate the potential of a market opportunity in more detail.

Factors that Influence Market Opportunities

To identify market opportunities, it's essential to understand the factors that influence them. These factors can vary depending on the product or service, industry, and market conditions.

One major factor in determining an opportunity is the customer's need or desire for a product or service. Customers seek solutions to problems they face, and businesses that can offer those solutions stand to gain a competitive edge.

Another factor influencing market opportunities is the potential for growth. A market with high growth prospects presents an opportunity for businesses to expand and increase their revenue streams.

It's also essential to consider the competitive landscape. Analyzing the market's existing players and their strategies can indicate potential gaps in the market that new businesses can exploit.

Furthermore, the regulatory and legal environment can significantly impact market opportunities. The regulations governing a particular industry can create barriers to entry, which businesses should weigh in their decision-making process.

Lastly, economic factors can influence market opportunities. The potential for a recession or economic downturn can impact consumer spending and businesses' ability to invest in growth.

Identifying these factors and analyzing how they apply to a specific market can help entrepreneurs determine the best course of action in pursuing market opportunities.

Challenges in Identifying Market Opportunities

Identifying and analyzing market opportunities is a crucial step in starting a successful business. However, this is easier said than done. One of the major challenges that entrepreneurs face is identifying the right market opportunities. Not all opportunities are created equal, and not all opportunities are suitable for every business.

The challenge in identifying market opportunities is that entrepreneurs must be able to differentiate between a good opportunity and a bad one. It's not just about finding an opportunity - it's about finding the right opportunity that is aligned with the business's strengths, weaknesses, vision, and values.

Moreover, entrepreneurs must also be able to identify the market gap that they can fill. This is not always easy, as the market is constantly changing, and what might have been a viable opportunity yesterday may not be the case today. Entrepreneurs must keep a finger on the pulse of the market and be willing to adapt and pivot as needed.

Another challenge in identifying market opportunities is understanding the competition. Entrepreneurs must research and analyze the competition to determine how they can differentiate themselves and offer something unique to the market. This requires a deep understanding of the market and the customers' needs and preferences.

Finally, entrepreneurs must also consider the risks and potential pitfalls of every opportunity. Every opportunity comes with risks, and it's important to evaluate and manage them effectively. This requires a strategic mindset and an ability to assess and mitigate risks.

Identifying and analyzing market opportunities is a challenge for every entrepreneur. By understanding the challenges and developing a strategic and adaptable approach, entrepreneurs can increase their chances of finding the right opportunity and building a successful business.

Market Research

The Significance of Market Research

The significance of market research cannot be overstated in the process of identifying and analyzing market opportunities. It is essential to research and understand the needs and desires of potential customers, as well as the characteristics of the market in which you plan to operate.

Market research provides valuable insights into your target market, including demographic information, purchasing behavior, and consumer preferences. This information can help you identify potential gaps in the market and opportunities for innovation.

Additionally, market research can inform your business decisions, such as pricing, product development, and marketing strategies. For example, understanding the competitive landscape of your market can help you position your products or services successfully.

However, it is crucial to conduct proper and unbiased market research. Biased research can lead to incorrect assumptions, poor business decisions, and missed opportunities. It is essential to approach market research with an open mind and use a variety of methods, including surveys, focus groups, and secondary research.

Market research is a crucial step in identifying and analyzing market opportunities. By researching and understanding your target market, you can develop successful business strategies that align with customer needs and preferences.

Conducting Market Research

After identifying a potential market opportunity, you must conduct market research to determine whether it is viable and worth pursuing. Market research involves gathering and analyzing data about your target customers, competitors, and industry trends.

To conduct market research, you can employ both primary and secondary research techniques. Primary research involves gathering data directly from the source through methods such as surveys, interviews, and observation. Secondary research involves analyzing existing data, such as government reports, industry publications, and competitor websites.

An important aspect of conducting market research is defining your target audience. This involves identifying the characteristics of your potential customers, such as age, gender, income, location, and interests. You can use this information to refine your marketing strategy and tailor your products or services to appeal to your target audience.

Another important component of market research is analyzing your competition. You can gain insight into your competition by researching their products or services, pricing strategies, marketing tactics, and customer reviews. Understanding the strengths and weaknesses of your competitors can help you position your business in the market and differentiate yourself from the competition.

Ultimately, the goal of conducting market research is to

determine the viability of a market opportunity and gather information that can inform your business strategy. By taking the time to conduct thorough market research, you can minimize risk and increase your chances of success as an entrepreneur.

Analyzing Market Research Data

Once you have gathered market research data, the next step is to analyze it thoroughly. This analysis is crucial because it provides insights into the needs and preferences of your target customers.

First, sort the data based on your research objectives. Separate the data that provides information about your target audience, the nature of the product or service, competitors, and market trends.

Next, look for patterns in the data. The goal is to identify trends and anomalies and use them to make informed decisions. Look for trends in customer preferences, behavior, buying habits, and satisfaction levels.

Identify the strengths and weaknesses of your competitors by analyzing their products or services offered, marketing strategies, pricing, and distribution channels. This analysis will enable you to position your product or service better than your competitors.

Finally, analyze the overall market trends. Determine if the market is growing, stagnant, or declining. Study the competition to identify where the market gaps lie. Evaluate if your product or service complements the existing market offerings or provides a unique value proposition that has little or no competition.

By analyzing market research data, you can make informed decisions that will ultimately contribute to the success of your business.

Understanding Competitors

Before starting a business, it is crucial to know what you are getting into. It is essential to understand your competitors to identify the gaps in the market and the opportunities you can explore.

Competitor analysis is an essential tool to gain insight into your competitors' strengths and weaknesses, allowing you to form a better understanding of how they operate and what makes them successful. It is an analysis of the products, services, and strategies of the competitors in your industry, providing a clear understanding of what they offer, how they engage with customers, and their business practices.

The first step to analyzing your competitors is to identify them. Start by conducting a search online, talking to industry experts, or attending trade shows. Once you have established your competitors, gather information about them through their website, their social media accounts, and their promotional materials.

Identifying your competitors' strengths and weaknesses is essential in gaining an understanding of what works and what doesn't work in your industry. You can use the SWOT analysis to evaluate their strengths, weaknesses, opportunities, and threats. This analysis will give you an overview of how they operate and what makes them stand out.

Observe how they interact with their customers, the products and services they offer, and their marketing strategies. It is also important to know your competitors' pricing strategy, how they operate, and their target audience.

Understanding your competitors' practices enables you to identify growth opportunities and how you can position yourself to fill gaps in the market. Knowing your competition also allows you to create realistic business goals and a plan of action to achieve them.

Competitor analysis is a critical aspect of market research. It provides insight into your competitors' strategies and enables you to position your business in a way that differentiates you from the competition. By understanding your competitors, you can create a business that offers unique and valuable products or services that appeal to your target audience.

Forecasting Market Trends

As an entrepreneur, one of your crucial tasks is identifying and forecasting market trends to stay ahead in the game. Market trends refer to the direction of the market, where it is headed, and its current underlying forces. Business owners who don't pay attention to industry trends risk missing out on opportunities or being caught off-guard by industry disruptions.

So, how do you forecast market trends? Here are some

steps to help you out:

Understand the market factors: To forecast market trends, you must know what drives them. Study the economic, political, social, and technological factors that affect your industry or niche. These factors will help you predict future trends that will shape your market.

Analyze existing data: Analyze existing market data to identify patterns, market fluctuations, and customer trends. Some useful sources of data include government reports, competitor's annual reports, social media trends, and industry-specific publications.

Conduct primary research: Conduct primary research by interacting with your customers, industry experts, and key players. Use surveys, focus groups, and one-on-one interviews to gain valuable insights. This will help you understand consumer preferences, current market dynamics, and the factors that influence buying decisions.

Use forecasting tools: Use forecasting tools to analyze past sales data and predict future ones. Such tools can spot patterns in sales data that are not visible to the human eye. They can also make predictions based on factors such as consumer preferences, demographic data, and economic indicators.

Forecasting market trends is an ongoing task that helps businesses stay relevant and competitive. By understanding market drivers, researching existing market data, conducting primary research, and using forecasting tools, entrepreneurs can predict future trends and stay ahead in the game.

Evaluating Market Opportunities

The Process of Evaluating Market Opportunities

The process of evaluating market opportunities requires a keen eye for detail and a deep understanding of market dynamics. It involves assessing the viability of various markets based on a set of criteria and determining which markets are worth pursuing.

One important step in evaluating market opportunities is to analyze the competition. This involves understanding the strengths and weaknesses of competitors and assessing how your product or service can differentiate itself in the market. By understanding what your competition lacks, you can provide solutions to customers that they cannot currently find.

Another aspect of evaluating market opportunities is to assess the size and growth potential of the market. This involves looking at factors such as population size, purchasing power, and disposable income among others. Analyzing historical trends and projecting future growth allows you to see if the market's potential will meet your business goals.

A thorough analysis of customer needs and preferences is also crucial in evaluating market opportunities. Surveys, focus groups and online reviews are great tools to gather information about what customers want and expect from products in your market segment. Answers gathered can be used to tailor your product or service so that it closely aligns with customer preferences.

Lastly, evaluating market opportunities involves calculating the potential costs and returns on investment. Creating a budget that includes every aspect of your business helps you to figure out the profits you expect from your venture. Once you have a clear understanding of the potential earnings, you can decide whether or not it meets your financial expectations.

SWOT Analysis

Evaluating market opportunities requires a thorough analysis of internal and external factors that can affect the success of a business. One of the most popular and effective tools used in evaluating opportunities is the SWOT analysis.

SWOT stands for Strengths, Weaknesses, Opportunities, and Threats. Strengths and weaknesses are internal factors that refer to the business's resources and capabilities. Meanwhile, opportunities and threats are external factors that refer to the market and industry conditions.

To conduct a SWOT analysis, the business owner needs to first identify their resources, including their employees, technology, and financial strength. They also need to examine their weaknesses, such as lack of experience or business systems. Once these factors are identified, they can be analyzed to determine opportunities for growth and areas that may pose a threat to the business.

Strengths and opportunities can be leveraged to create a competitive advantage in the market, while weaknesses and threats can be addressed to minimize risk and prevent failure.

When evaluating opportunities, it is essential to look at the current market trends and competitive landscape. Understanding the market segment, customer behavior, and industry forces allows the business owner to identify the gaps and opportunities in the market.

Thus, conducting a SWOT analysis to evaluate market opportunities is a critical step in building a successful business.

Measuring Market Potential

In order to identify viable market opportunities, it is essential to assess the market potential of each opportunity. Measuring market potential means evaluating the possible sales volume for a particular product or service in a given market.

A variety of factors must be taken into consideration when measuring market potential, including market size, target customer demographics, and competitive landscape. It is important to research not just the overall size of the market, but also the specific segments of the market that align with your product or service.

Once you have a clear understanding of the market size and target customer demographics, it is important to evaluate the competitive landscape. This includes identifying existing businesses in the market and analyzing their strengths and weaknesses. Understanding the competitive landscape can help you identify gaps in the market and determine if there is room for your offering.

In addition to evaluating the competitive landscape, it is important to assess any potential barriers to entry, such as regulatory requirements or high startup costs. This can help you determine if there are any major challenges to entering the market and if it is financially feasible to do so.

Finally, it is important to consider any potential market trends and disruptions that could impact the market over time. This includes technological advancements, changes in consumer behavior, and economic trends. A comprehensive understanding of the market potential will help you make informed decisions about which opportunities to pursue and how to position your offering within the market.

Identifying Key Success Factors

When analyzing a potential market opportunity, there are a few key success factors that business owners must consider to determine if it is worth pursuing. These factors include:

Market size and potential - An opportunity with a large and growing market is more likely to lead to success than one with a small or shrinking market.

Competitive landscape - Research the competition and determine how your business can differentiate itself from similar offerings in the market.

Customer needs - Identify the specific needs of your target market and determine if your product or service can meet those needs.

Barriers to entry - Assess the level of difficulty and cost associated with entering the market. Is there a high barrier to entry, making it more difficult for new competitors to enter?

Regulatory environment - Understand the laws and regulations surrounding the industry, and determine if they will have an impact on your ability to enter and compete in the market.

By carefully evaluating these key success factors, you can determine if a market opportunity is viable and create a plan to capitalize on it. Remember that success is not guaranteed, but conducting thorough research and analysis can increase your chances of success.

Factors to Consider in Choosing a Market Opportunity.

When identifying and analyzing a potential market opportunity, there are various factors to consider to determine whether the opportunity is worth pursuing. Here are some factors to take into account:

Market Size and Potential: Evaluate the size of the target market and the potential for growth. Consider whether the market is growing or shrinking and whether there are any major trends or changes that may affect the potential growth of the market.

Competition: Analyze the level of competition in the market, including the number of competitors and their market share. Consider the strengths and weaknesses of each competitor, as well as any barriers to entry that may exist.

Customer Needs and Preferences: Understand the needs and preferences of your potential customers. What are their pain points and what solutions are they seeking? Determine if your product or service aligns with their needs.

Economic Factors: Analyze the economic factors that may impact the market, such as the overall economic climate and any relevant government regulations or policies. Consider how these factors may affect the demand for your product or service.

Resource Requirements: Assess the resources required to enter the market, such as financial capital, personnel, and technology. Evaluate whether your business has the necessary resources to compete in the market.

By evaluating these factors, you can determine whether the market opportunity is viable and whether it aligns with your business goals and capabilities. Taking the time to conduct a comprehensive market analysis can help you make informed decisions and increase your chances of success.

Developing a Business Plan

Creating a Mission and Vision Statement

Defining your purpose

Developing a Business Plan
Defining the purpose of your business is the first step in creating a mission and vision statement. Your purpose provides direction and motivates you to work towards a common goal. In defining your purpose, ask yourself why you want to start your business. What is your passion? What problem does your business solve? What value will your business provide to your customers?

Once you have a clear idea of your purpose, create a statement that summarizes it concisely. Your purpose statement should be a few sentences that accurately capture the essence of your business. A well-crafted purpose statement sets the tone for your entire business plan and helps keep you focused on your goals.

To develop your purpose statement, consider the following:

Who are your customers, and what problem are you solving for them?

What makes your business unique or different from your competitors?

How will your business impact your community or industry?

What values are important to your business, and how will you uphold them?

With these questions in mind, write a draft of your purpose statement. Be clear and concise, avoiding jargon or buzzwords. Your statement should be easy to understand and memorable, yet comprehensive enough to convey the essence of your business.

Remember, your purpose statement should be authentic to you and your business. It's the foundation upon which you will build everything else, so take the time to craft a purpose statement that truly captures your passion and goals. With a strong purpose statement in place, you'll be better equipped to create the rest of your business plan, including your vision statement, marketing strategy, and financial projections.

Creating a unique value proposition

Developing a Business Plan
A business plan serves as a roadmap for any venture, outlining its goals and how it intends to achieve them. The mission and vision statement is a crucial part of this plan, as it provides clarity about what the business stands for and what it aims to achieve. But to differentiate oneself from competitors in the marketplace, a unique value proposition is a must. The value proposition defines the problem being solved, the target market, and how it provides a better solution than other competitors in the market.

A unique value proposition is a concise statement that distinguishes the business from the competition by highlighting its unique benefits. It is a clear and compelling statement that explains what the business does and why it is better than others.

To create a unique value proposition, start by asking yourself these questions:

What problem or need does your product or service solve, and for whom?
What is your unique approach, feature, or benefit that sets you apart from competitors?
How does your product or service improve the life or work of your customers?

A strong value proposition has four key components:

It is clear and concise.
It focuses on the customer and their needs.
It distinguishes the business from its competitors.
It communicates the unique benefit and value that the business provides.

Crafting a strong value proposition can take time and effort, but it is critical to the success of any business. It allows the initial communication with potential customers to be clear about its purpose, and its competitive advantage. With a strong value proposition, entrepreneurs can create a foundation that sets their business up for success.

Identifying target customers

Before you can create a mission and vision statement, it's essential to identify your target customers. Your target customers are the people who are most likely to be interested in your product or service. A lot of new business owners make the mistake of thinking that everyone is their target customer. But the reality is, no product or service is suitable for everyone.

To identify your target customers, you need to conduct thorough market research. This research will help you to understand things like:

- Who your ideal customer is
- What problems they're facing that your product or service can solve
- What their needs and wants are
- How much they're willing to pay for your product or service

Some ways to conduct market research include:

- Online surveys
- Focus groups
- Customer interviews
- Social media listening
- Competitor analysis

By understanding your target customer, you can create a mission and vision statement that speaks directly to them. Your mission statement should be a short, clear statement that describes your business's purpose and what sets it apart from competitors. Your vision statement, on the other hand, should describe your long-term goals for your business.

Understanding your target customers is critical to the success of your business. It helps you to create a mission and vision statement that will resonate with your ideal customer and set you apart from competitors in the market.

Establishing business goals

Once you have established your purpose and values, the next step in creating a mission and vision statement is to set specific business goals. Goals provide direction and purpose, and help you make decisions that are aligned with your overall vision.

To establish business goals, start by identifying the key areas of your business that you want to develop. Depending on where your business is at, these might include increasing revenue, expanding your customer base, improving your marketing strategy, or developing new products or services.

Once you have identified your key areas, set specific, measurable goals for each. For example, if you want to increase revenue, you might set a goal to increase sales by a certain percentage within a specific timeframe. If you want to expand your customer base, you might set a goal to acquire a certain number of new customers each month.

When setting goals, it's important to make sure they are realistic and achievable. Consider your available resources, your current market position, and any potential obstacles you might face.

In addition to setting goals for your business as a whole, it can also be helpful to set goals for individual team members. This helps ensure that everyone is working towards the same objectives, and gives team members a sense of ownership and accountability.

Setting specific business goals is an essential step in creating a mission and vision statement that will guide your business towards success. By establishing clear objectives that are aligned with your values and purpose, you can make informed decisions and achieve meaningful progress.

Crafting a mission and vision statement

Before you start your business, it's essential to clearly articulate what you stand for and why you exist. Crafting a mission and vision statement can help you do just that. Your mission statement should provide a concise and compelling summary of your organization's goals, values, and purpose. On the other hand, your vision statement should reflect your long-term aspirations and achievements in the future.

When creating a mission statement, it's essential to consider what makes your business unique. Ask yourself questions such as, "What makes us stand out from our competition?" or "How do our products or services improve the lives of our customers?" By answering these questions, you'll be better positioned to come up with an authentic and distinctive mission statement.

It's also crucial to keep your mission statement concise and straightforward. Ideally, it should be just a sentence or two that can be easily remembered and communicated. Above all, your mission statement should be inspiring and motivating. It should help you and your team stay focused on what is essential and keep pushing forward.

While a mission statement focuses on the present, a vision statement is all about the future. It's essentially a roadmap that reflects where you're headed and what you want to achieve in the long term. Therefore, it should be aspirational and inspiring.

When crafting your vision statement, it's essential to be specific and measurable. Instead of making broad and vague statements, think about concrete, achievable goals that will help you get to where you want to be. Consider factors like revenue, product offerings, or market share.

As with your mission statement, it's essential to keep your vision statement concise and easy to remember. It should be a rallying cry that motivates you and your team to work towards a common goal. By crafting a clear and compelling mission and vision statement, you'll be better positioned to develop a successful business plan that reflects your goals and values.

Conducting Market Research

Understanding industry competitors

Developing a Business Plan

One of the critical modules of market research when creating a business plan is to understand the competition. This section will help you analyze your competition and show you how to use the information to your advantage.

Understanding your competition is crucial to your success, and it starts with identifying your direct and indirect competitors. Direct competitors are those businesses that offer similar products or services and target the same audience as yours. On the other hand, indirect competitors are businesses that offer alternative products or services but still target the same audience.

Once you have identified your competitors, the next step is to analyze and evaluate their strengths and weaknesses. This will allow you to understand how they operate, their pricing strategies, marketing tactics, and customer experience. You can use this information to identify gaps in the market and develop innovative solutions that give you a competitive edge.

It's important to note that analyzing your competitors isn't about copying their strategies, nor is it about undermining them. Rather, it's about understanding their approach and seeing how you can differentiate yourself. By doing so, you can create a unique selling proposition (USP), which makes your business stand out and attract your ideal customers.

In addition, evaluating your competitors is an ongoing process that requires consistency and a willingness to learn. It's not enough to analyze your competition before you launch your business and forget about them afterward. Monitoring your competitors' activities regularly can help you stay ahead of the curve and develop a strategy that ensures your business remains relevant and competitive.

Understanding industry competitors is an essential part of market research when developing a business plan. It allows you to identify gaps in the market and develop a unique selling proposition that differentiates your business. Moreover, regularly monitoring your competitors can help you stay ahead of the curve and adapt to market changes.

Analyzing target market trends

Developing a Business Plan
To create a successful business plan, you need to conduct thorough market research to identify the needs and wants of your target market. Analyzing the current trends in your target market is a crucial step in understanding your potential customer base and staying ahead of competitors.

Start by identifying your target market segment and researching their behavior, preferences, and needs. Look for any emerging trends that might impact your industry and be proactive in adapting to those changes.

To analyze target market trends, you can use different tools and resources such as online surveys, focus groups, and social media to gather data about your potential customers. Analyze the data collected, and use it to identify changes that might be taking place in your industry.

Additionally, you can use competitor analysis to identify their target markets and the strategies they use to attract customers. Compare their products and services to yours and, identify gaps that exist, and areas where you can excel.

Finally, stay up-to-date with the latest technology and platforms that might present new opportunities to reach customers. By analyzing market trends, you will be able to make informed decisions that can help you stay ahead of the competition and make your business successful.

Assessing market demand

Developing a Business Plan
Assessing the demand for a product or service requires in-depth research, as well as a clear understanding of the target market. The goal of market research is to identify the needs and preferences of potential customers and determine whether there is potential demand for the product or service.

To assess market demand, entrepreneurs must start by identifying potential customers and their characteristics, such as age, income, and location. They can use various methods to gather information, including surveys, focus groups, and online research.

Additionally, entrepreneurs can analyze industry trends and competition to gain insights into how the market is evolving and identify potential gaps that the product or service could fill. Another key consideration is pricing strategy and whether the business can compete effectively with other players in the market.

Assessing market demand is a critical step in developing a successful business plan. By understanding the needs and preferences of potential customers, entrepreneurs can ensure that their product or service is well-positioned to meet market demand and ultimately achieve long-term success.

Conducting customer surveys

Developing a Business Plan
Before launching a new product or service, it's vital to conduct market research to ensure its viability. One of the most effective methods of market research is conducting customer surveys.

Customer surveys allow entrepreneurs to obtain valuable insights into customer demographics, purchasing behavior, and preferences. These insights are essential in guiding product development and marketing strategy.

To conduct customer surveys, entrepreneurs must first define their target audience and develop a set of open-ended and closed-ended questions that address their research objectives. Closed-ended questions are limited to specific answers, while open-ended questions permit more extended answers.

Entrepreneurs can conduct customer surveys through various channels such as email, social media, or phone. They should also consider survey incentives to encourage customer participation.

Once the data is collected, entrepreneurs must analyze it for patterns and trends that reveal customer needs, preferences, and behaviors. This analysis should guide product development, marketing messaging, and customer engagement strategies.

Customer surveys are a powerful tool for conducting market research and obtaining valuable insights into customer behavior and preferences. Entrepreneurs who leverage this tool and apply the insights gained in their strategies stand a better chance of success in their businesses.

Analyzing data and making informed decisions

Developing a Business Plan: Conducting Market Research - Analyzing Data and Making Informed Decisions

After collecting data during the market research process, it's time to analyze the data and make informed decisions. The analysis of this data can provide valuable insight into the industry, target audience, competition, and trends. Entrepreneurs can use this information to make informed decisions about product development, pricing, marketing, and sales strategies, and other aspects of their business plans.

One of the primary tools used for analyzing market research data is the SWOT analysis, which stands for strengths, weaknesses, opportunities, and threats. It's a useful way to identify internal and external factors that can impact the success of a business.

When analyzing market data, it's essential to look for patterns and trends. For instance, use SWOT analysis to group data based on its relevance. Identify strengths and opportunities that suggest a specific approach, and then find ways to leverage these factors for your business. Conversely, identify weaknesses and threats that should be mitigated or avoided.

It's also important to keep in mind the context of the data collected. A single data point may not be significant, but when viewed in the context of larger trends, it can become more meaningful. Entrepreneurs must look beyond the specific data points and consider how they fit into the overall picture.

Analyzing data is critical to make informed decisions when creating a business plan. The SWOT analysis provides a useful framework for identifying internal and external factors that can impact the success of a business. By looking for patterns and trends and considering the context, entrepreneurs can use market research data to create effective strategies for their businesses.

Developing a Marketing and Sales Strategy

Identifying marketing channels

Once you have conducted thorough research on your target audience, it's time to identify the marketing channels that will allow you to reach them effectively. This step is all about understanding your customers' behavior and preferences.

One of the most effective ways to reach your target audience is through social media platforms such as Facebook, Instagram, Twitter, LinkedIn, and more. Social media channels can help you build brand awareness, advertise your products or services, connect with potential customers and establish yourself as an expert in your niche.

In addition to social media, you can also leverage other online channels such as search engine optimization (SEO), content creation, email marketing, paid advertising, and more. Similarly, offline channels such as events, print ads, direct mail marketing, and radio or television ads can also prove useful depending on your specific target audience and business goals.
Ultimately, your decision on which marketing channels to use will depend on your target audience, your business goals, and your available resources. By understanding and selecting the best channels to reach your target audience, you will be well on your way to achieving your marketing and sales objectives.

Creating a brand identity

Developing a Business Plan

Your brand identity is a combination of things that make your business unique. It includes your logo, color scheme, typography, tone of voice, advertising, and packaging. Your brand identity is essential to your success because it's how people recognize and remember your business.

To create a brand identity that resonates with your target market, you should start by conducting market research. Find out what your potential customers need and want, and use that information to develop a unique brand identity that speaks directly to them.

Your brand identity should be consistent across all channels, including your website, social media, packaging, and advertising. Consistency helps build trust and makes your business more memorable.

When creating your brand identity, keep in mind that your target market should be at the forefront of your decisions. What do they want to see and hear? What values do they hold? Use that information to guide your branding decisions.

Your visual identity - the logo, colors, and typography - should be appealing to your target market and reflect your business's personality. The tone of voice you use in your marketing materials should also resonate with your target market.

Creating a strong brand identity is an important component of your marketing and sales strategy. It helps differentiate your business from your competitors and makes your business more memorable to your target market.

Defining a pricing strategy

After conducting market research, it's time to define your pricing strategy. Pricing is a crucial element of your overall marketing plan, as it affects how customers perceive your brand, the sales volume, and ultimately, the revenue you generate.

The first step is to understand the customer. Identify their pain points and compare your product or service with that of competitors. Additionally, understand who your target audience is, and their buying behavior. Once you have their preferences and characteristics that are essential in determining pricing, extrapolate their perceived value of your product or service.

After identifying your customers' perceived value, consider your production costs, such as materials, labor, and overhead, and use this to calculate a base price. Marketing strategies, such as discounts, carts, promotions, and customer service, must follow the pricing strategy to cater to the target audience.

Consider price elasticity, which determines whether a price increase or decrease would affect consumer demand. Price elasticity is affected by factors such as product availability, competitor pricing, income, switching costs, and perceived value. Through this, you can assess when demand is elastic or inelastic and, as a result, determine whether to increase or decrease prices.

Pricing is not static but, instead, requires continuous adjustments based on changes in the market, competitors, and consumer preferences. Keep track of market trends, conduct market surveys, and perform price testing to determine optimal pricing.

Investing in the right marketing strategy and pricing strategy can translate to increased brand visibility, loyal customers, and increased sales volume. It's important to remember that your pricing strategy must align with your business's mission, long-term goals, and the perceived value of your product or service.

Building a sales funnel

A sales funnel is a significant part of any successful marketing and sales strategy. It is the process in which potential customers go through before they become paying customers. Building a sales funnel involves understanding consumer behavior, identifying their needs and pain points, and creating a journey that addresses them.

The first step in building a sales funnel is understanding the target audience. A business owner must invest time and effort into researching their customers' demographics, behaviors, interests, and problems. With this information, they can create buyer personas that represent their ideal customer. This knowledge is crucial in creating a personalized experience for customers that will increase the chances of them following through and purchasing the product.

The next step is creating awareness of the product. This can be done through advertising, content marketing, social media marketing, or any other marketing strategy that works best for the business owner. The aim is to create a message that speaks to the buyers' pain points and positions the product as the solution.

The next stage of the funnel is consideration. At this point, the potential customer has expressed an interest in the product and is considering whether or not to make a purchase. Providing a free trial, a demo, or a consultation can help in persuading the customer.

After consideration is the decision stage. At this point, the potential customer converts into a paying customer. Business owners must make the decision process as frictionless as possible to increase the conversion rate. This can be done through streamlined purchasing processes or providing clear pricing information.

The final stage of the funnel is post-purchase. At this point, customer satisfaction is crucial. Business owners must ensure they provide excellent customer service and resolve any issues that may arise. Happy customers will not only become loyal customers but can also drive referrals and positive word-of-mouth marketing.

Building a sales funnel is critical to attracting and retaining customers. Business owners must understand their target audience, create awareness and consideration, make the decision process as frictionless as possible, and provide excellent post-purchase customer service.

Implementing and measuring marketing efforts

As an entrepreneur, it's fundamental to have a clear understanding of how you will market and sell your product or service. Even if you have a great product, if you don't have an effective marketing strategy in place, it's unlikely that you'll be able to generate sales. In this subsection, we'll discuss how to implement and measure marketing efforts to ensure you're on the right track.

The first step is to identify your target audience. Who are your ideal customers? What are their pain points, challenges, and desires? You need to understand what motivates them to buy products or services like yours. Once you've identified your target audience, you can craft a messaging strategy that resonates with them.

The next step is to determine which channels you'll use to reach your target audience. There are many channels available, including social media, email marketing, paid advertising, content marketing, and more. It's important to select the channels that your target audience uses most frequently.

Once you've identified your channels, it's time to create content that will engage and convert your audience. Your content should align with your messaging strategy and should provide value to your target audience. You should also consider the format of your content, such as blog articles, videos, social media posts, and so on.

Measuring the success of your marketing efforts is critical. You need to know what's working and what's not so that you can adjust your strategy accordingly. There are many metrics you can track, including website traffic, social media engagement, email open rates, and conversion rates. You should regularly review your metrics to identify what's working and what's not.

Developing a marketing and sales strategy is crucial to the success of any business. By identifying your target audience, selecting the right channels, creating engaging content, and measuring your success, you can build a marketing strategy that generates sales and helps you achieve your business goals.

Building a Strong Team

Identifying the Right People

Knowing the Importance of a Good Fit

When it comes to building a successful business, much of the conversation revolves around finding the right people for your team. However, it's not just about finding people with the necessary skills or experience. Rather, it's about finding individuals who are a good fit for your specific company culture and vision. Why is finding the right fit so important?

For one, hiring someone who isn't a good fit can lead to a host of problems down the line. This could include conflict with other team members, low morale, or difficulty achieving shared goals. On the other hand, when you find people who are the right fit for your company, you can expect to see better job satisfaction, improved productivity, and more effective collaboration.

So how do you identify the right fit for your team? Start by getting clear on what your company culture is and what values are most important to you. For example, if open and honest communication is a top priority, you'll want to look for individuals who share that value. Additionally, think about the specific skills and traits that are necessary for each position, and look for candidates who possess those.

It's also important to look for behavioral indicators during the interview process. For example, you can ask questions that gauge a candidate's work style, personality, and approach to problem-solving. Additionally, consider setting up a trial period where candidates can work with your team on a temporary basis to see how well they fit in.

Finding people who are a good fit for your company culture is essential for building a strong team. By taking the time to identify the right people and assess their fit, you can set your business up for long-term success.

Leveraging Personality Assessments

Assembling a team is a significant step in running a business. A team that is composed of individuals who possess a wide range of skills and expertise is often a key factor in business success. However, skills and expertise could not be the only factors you consider in choosing your team members. Understanding the personality traits of your potential team members is equally critical. You'll want to create a team that is not only knowledgeable and highly skilled but also has personalities that complement each other.

Personality assessments are a reliable tool for identifying these traits. These tests provide insights into the psychological makeup of individuals, determining how they perceive the world, their motivations, and behaviors. You'll want to understand how your potential team members handle stress, how they prefer to communicate, and what their emotional intelligence levels are, among other factors.

One popular personality assessment tool is the Myers-Briggs Type Indicator (MBTI). The MBTI is a self-reported test that categorizes individuals into one of sixteen personality types based on how they perceive the world, make decisions, and interact with others. Other personality assessment frameworks include the Big Five personality traits, the DiSC assessment, and the Enneagram, amongst others.

Before selecting your team members, ensure to have them complete a personality assessment. It helps you have a deep understanding of who they are, which will make it easier for you to determine their roles in your business. A team composed of individuals who understand each other's personalities will be more cohesive and better suited to work on projects together.

Creating Job Descriptions that Attract Top Talent

Building a Strong Team
Crafting effective job descriptions is essential to attracting the right people to your team. A well-written job description clearly outlines the duties, responsibilities, and qualifications required for the position. It should also convey the mission, vision, and values of the company, allowing potential candidates to determine if they align with your organization.

To create effective job descriptions, start with a clear understanding of the role you are filling. Consider the skills, experience, and personality traits needed for success in the position. Think about what motivates top talent and what sets your company apart from its competitors.

Use an attention-grabbing title to pique the interest of potential candidates. Then, clearly describe the responsibilities and duties associated with the role in a way that is both informative and engaging. Be sure to highlight any unique benefits or perks associated with working at your company.

In addition to outlining job requirements, be sure to include information about your company culture, your mission and values, and any opportunities for career growth and development. This will attract candidates who are not only qualified but also share your values and are excited about the opportunity to contribute to your company's success.

When crafting your job descriptions, it's important to be specific and avoid using vague or undefined terms. Use action verbs to clearly outline the responsibilities of the position and highlight the desired outcomes. Avoid overly technical jargon and be sure to clearly state the qualifications required for the role.

Remember, job descriptions should be a reflection of your company and the type of people you want to attract. Invest time and effort in creating job descriptions that effectively communicate your expectations and attract the right candidates to help your business succeed.

Conducting Effective Interviews

Building a Strong Team: Identifying the Right People
When it comes to building a strong team, one of the most important steps is identifying the right people for the job. This starts with conducting effective interviews.

The interview process is not just about determining whether a candidate has the necessary skills and experience for the role. It's also about assessing their fit with your company culture, their motivation and drive, and their ability to work well with others on your team.

To conduct effective interviews, start by creating a list of questions that will help you assess these different aspects of a candidate's suitability. This might include technical questions related to the role, as well as behavioural questions that reveal their approach to problem-solving, conflict resolution, and teamwork.

During the interview itself, try to create a comfortable and open atmosphere where candidates feel free to elaborate on their responses, ask questions, and share their own ideas and experiences. This will help you get a more complete picture of their personality and work style.

Throughout the process, it's important to stay mindful of your own biases and assumptions. Take care to ensure that you are evaluating candidates objectively, based solely on their qualifications, experiences, and suitability for the role.

In the end, the goal of a successful interview process should be to identify the candidates who have the potential to be a great fit for your team and your business, both now and in the future. By conducting interviews that are thorough, well-planned, and unbiased, you will be better equipped to build a strong team that can help you achieve your business goals.

Using Background Checks and References to Validate Your Hire

Building a Strong Team

When it comes to building a successful business, choosing the right team is essential. Hiring the wrong person can have serious consequences, including decreased productivity, lost revenue, and even legal issues. Therefore, it's essential to have a reliable hiring process in place that includes thorough background checks and reference gathering to validate your hire.

The first step in validating your hire is to conduct a comprehensive background check. This check should cover criminal history, employment and education verification, and reference checks. Criminal history checks can uncover any past criminal activity that may affect the candidate's suitability for the job. Employment and education verification ensures that the candidate's stated qualifications and experience match their actual history. Finally, reference checks allow you to get detailed feedback from previous employers, coworkers, and other references.

When conducting reference checks, it's essential to ask the right questions to get a clear picture of the candidate's character and work ethic. Some key questions to ask may include:

- Can you describe the candidate's work style?
- What were some of the candidate's biggest accomplishments while working with you?
- How did the candidate handle challenging or difficult situations?
- Would you rehire the candidate, and why or why not?

By conducting a thorough background check and reference gathering process, you can gain more confidence in your hiring decisions and increase the likelihood of building a strong, effective team. Additionally, it's crucial to keep in mind that your hiring process should be fair and unbiased, and you should comply with all relevant laws and regulations.

Training and Developing Your Team

Creating a Culture of Learning

Building a Strong Team
As an entrepreneur, it's important to constantly evaluate the skill sets within your team and identify areas where growth and development are needed. Creating a culture of learning throughout your organization not only helps develop your team's talents but also leads to continued business success.

When it comes to implementing a culture of learning there are a few key strategies to keep in mind. First, it's essential to provide ongoing training opportunities for your team, including both formal and informal sessions. These can include workshops, seminars, and online courses, as well as mentoring relationships with more experienced team members. Encouraging team members to share their knowledge and expertise with others in the organization creates a collaborative environment where learning is promoted at all levels.

A second strategy for creating a culture of learning is to make personal and professional development a priority for all team members. This includes setting goals, providing regular feedback on performance, and recognizing achievements. Providing resources such as books, articles, and podcasts, and creating opportunities for team members to attend conferences and networking events, encourages a mindset of continuous learning and growth.

Finally, it's important to lead by example and model the behavior you want to see from your team. As a founder or CEO, investing in your own learning and development sends a clear message to team members that ongoing growth and learning are valued within the organization.

By creating a culture of learning within your team, you not only develop the skills and talents necessary for continued business success but also create a positive and supportive environment where team members are encouraged to learn and grow together.

Providing Opportunities for Growth and Advancement

As a successful entrepreneur, one of the keys to building a strong team is providing opportunities for growth and advancement. When your team members feel like they have opportunities to learn and develop new skills, they are more likely to be engaged and committed to your business.

There are several ways to provide opportunities for growth and advancement within your team. One option is to offer regular training and development programs. These might include in-house training sessions, attending industry conferences, or enrolling team members in accredited courses or certifications.

Another way to encourage growth and advancement is to set clear career paths for your team members. This might involve setting up a promotion track or offering opportunities for lateral movement within the organization. It's important to communicate these opportunities clearly and regularly with your team members, so they know what they need to do to progress in their role.

Mentorship programs can also be an effective way to

support the growth and development of your team members. Pairing less experienced team members with more senior members of staff can provide valuable guidance and support, as well as helping to build a stronger sense of teamwork and camaraderie within your organization.

Ultimately, providing opportunities for growth and advancement is a win-win for both your business and your team members. By investing in your staff and helping them to develop new skills and advance their careers, you'll be building a more committed and engaged workforce, while also ensuring that your business is well-positioned for future growth and success.

Implementing Ongoing Training and Development Programs

Building a Strong Team
Implementing Ongoing Training and Development Programs

Training and development are essential components of building a strong team. After identifying the right people to join your team, it is necessary to provide them with the necessary skills to assist them in performing their tasks effectively. The provision of training and development programs should be ongoing to ensure that your team remains competitive and that they remain relevant to the changes in your industry.

One way to implement ongoing training and development programs is through a mentorship program. A mentorship program can help your team members become more knowledgeable about their work, improve their skills and increase productivity. Mentors can be chosen from your experienced staff members who can provide guidance, advice and support to the team as needed.

Another way to implement ongoing training and development programs is through workshops and seminars. These can be organized either externally or internally to educate team members on new trends and changes in the industry. Team members can also be exposed to new technologies, which can help them adapt better to changes in the industry.

Additionally, cross-training can be implemented to provide team members with new learning and development opportunities. Cross-training can help your team members develop additional skills and knowledge, which can be beneficial in times of employee absenteeism or to assist team members to work together more effectively.

It is important to monitor and evaluate the effectiveness of the training and development programs. This can help identify areas that need improvement and the areas that have been effective in providing the necessary skills and knowledge to team members. Regular feedback sessions can be held with the team members to understand the impact of the training and development programs and how additional improvements can be made.

Utilizing Mentoring and Coaching Strategies

As a business owner, investing in your team's training and development is essential. Every employee brings their own unique set of strengths and weaknesses to the table, and it's up to you to develop their potential fully.

One powerful way to develop employees is through mentoring and coaching strategies. By assigning mentors and coaches to your team, you give them a unique opportunity to learn and accelerate their professional growth.

Mentoring is an effective way to guide your employees' career development. It involves matching your team member with someone who can offer guidance in areas such as leadership, communication, or specific job skills. A mentor can offer insights, feedback, and support while helping to nurture the employee's career trajectory.

Coaching, on the other hand, is more focused on specific task-oriented goals. A coach helps the team member address specific challenges or develop specific abilities such as public speaking, sales, or time management. Coaching sessions may be one-time events focused on a particular need or may be ongoing, addressing multiple goals over an extended period.

Integrating mentoring and coaching strategies into your team's training and development plan can create a lasting impact on your business's overall success. These strategies help promote an environment in which employee growth is a top priority, and you empower your team to reach their full potential while driving business results.

Encouraging Peer-to-Peer Learning and Collaboration

In addition to identifying the right people and providing

effective communication, it's also essential to foster learning and collaboration within your team. As a business owner, it's your responsibility to ensure that your team has the tools and resources they need to succeed, and this includes enabling peer-to-peer learning and collaboration.

One effective way to encourage peer-to-peer learning within your team is to establish cross-functional projects or teams. By bringing together individuals from different departments, you can create opportunities for employees to learn from one another, gain new skills, and work together to solve problems. This can also help to break down silos within your organization and promote a more cohesive overall culture.

Another effective way to foster peer-to-peer learning and collaboration within your team is to establish a mentorship program. By connecting more experienced employees with newer team members, you can help to facilitate knowledge sharing and skill development. This can also help to promote a sense of community within your organization and provide employees with a support system as they navigate their roles.

Encouraging ongoing communication and feedback is also crucial for facilitating peer-to-peer learning within your team. By regularly soliciting input and ideas from team members, you can create an environment that values open dialogue and encourages the sharing of knowledge and expertise.

Ultimately, training and developing your team is an ongoing process. By fostering peer-to-peer learning and collaboration within your organization, you can help to promote continuous growth and improvement, both individually and as a team.

Communicating Effectively with Your Team

Establishing Open Lines of Communication

Building a Strong Team: Communicating Effectively with Your Team - Establishing Open Lines of Communication

Communication is an essential component of a successful business. As an entrepreneur, you need to establish open lines of communication with your team members to foster collaboration and ensure everyone is on the same page. Establishing open lines of communication involves:

Encouraging Expression

One of the primary ways of establishing open lines of communication is by fostering an environment that encourages team members to voice their opinions, ask questions, or make suggestions. You can create an environment that allows for open expression by limiting hierarchical structures, reducing power dynamics, and creating opportunities for everyone to be heard. When team members feel their input is valued, they become more invested in the success of the business.

Utilizing Technology

In today's technology-driven age, various tools and software can improve communication within the team. For example, enterprise messaging applications like Slack, Trello, and Asana allow team members to share ideas, communicate project progress, and collaborate on tasks in real-time. Utilizing technology solutions can help team members stay connected, track progress, and flag any challenges or issues that may arise.

Empowering Employees

When team members feel empowered, they are more willing to participate in communication efforts. You can achieve this by giving them responsibility, recognizing their achievements, and providing them with opportunities to grow in the company. Empowering your team members can also mean taking a step back and allowing them to make decisions, take ownership of projects, and lead initiatives.

Providing Constructive Feedback

Finally, as the team leader, it is crucial to provide constructive feedback to your team members regularly. Feedback creates accountability, helps in identifying areas of improvement, and boosts morale when things are going well. Providing feedback requires consistency, clarity, and specificity. Focus on highlighting areas of improvement and commend team members on their successes.

Establishing open lines of communication is critical to building a strong team. By fostering an environment that encourages expression, utilizing technology, empowering employees, and providing constructive feedback, you can establish a communication framework that promotes collaboration, improves productivity, and ensures the team is working towards the same goal.

Giving and Receiving Feedback Effectively

In order to build a strong team, effective communication is key. An essential aspect of communication is giving and receiving feedback. As a business owner, you need to provide constructive feedback to your team members on a regular basis. It helps them understand their areas of improvement and motivates them to perform better. However, giving feedback is not always easy. It requires tact, sensitivity, and empathy.

Firstly, start by creating a safe environment to give feedback. Ensure that your employees feel comfortable expressing themselves and understand that criticism is intended to help them improve. Be clear and specific about the feedback you want to give and explain why it is important. Avoid using negative language or implying that their actions are a reflection of their character.

When providing feedback, it is important to focus on behavior rather than personality traits. Discuss the specific actions that are of concern and provide examples based on factual observations. Use the 'sandwich method' to give feedback. Start and end with positive comments while offering constructive criticism in the middle. Avoid being critical of everything and focus on key areas that need improvement.

On the other hand, receiving feedback is equally important for personal growth. As a business owner, it's important to lead by example and set the tone for feedback acceptance. Actively listen to the feedback given and ask clarifying questions to ensure you fully grasp the situation. Thank the individual for their feedback and take some time to process it before responding. Responding defensively is never helpful in a feedback situation.

Incorporating regular feedback mechanisms into your business culture can maintain open lines of communication between you and your employees. Additionally, encourage ongoing self-initiated feedback between your employees to create a culture of continuous improvement.

Effective communication through feedback is an essential element of building a strong team. When handled with care and respect, it leads to better performance, employee satisfaction, and business growth.

Encouraging Constructive Conflict and Empathy

Building a Strong Team
Effective communication is critical in building a strong team. You need to ensure that everyone is on the same page, that there are no misunderstandings, and that everyone feels heard and valued. But communication is more than just talking and listening; it's about creating an environment where constructive conflict can thrive, and empathy can flourish.

Constructive conflict is a healthy part of any team dynamic. It encourages everyone to challenge their assumptions and promotes creativity and innovation. However, it can be challenging to encourage constructive conflict without letting things get out of hand. As a leader, you need to ensure that everyone feels comfortable expressing their opinion and making suggestions. You can do this by creating ground rules for discussions, ensuring that everyone has an opportunity to speak, and acknowledging and thanking people for their contributions.

Empathy is also essential in effective communication. It's

about understanding and relating to people's feelings and perspectives. When you practice empathy, you create a space where people feel understood and valued, which in turn fosters a sense of community and encourages teamwork.

One way to promote empathy is to actively listen to people. Show interest in what they have to say, and don't interrupt or dismiss their ideas. Another way to promote empathy is to encourage people to share their experiences and perspectives. When people understand each other's backgrounds and motivations, they are more likely to work together effectively.

Finally, it's crucial to remember that effective communication is a two-way street. As a leader, you need to encourage your team to communicate with you openly and honestly. This means being receptive to feedback and criticism and using it to improve yourself and your leadership style.

Effective communication is critical in building a strong team, and it involves creating an environment that encourages constructive conflict and empathy. As a leader, it's your responsibility to create ground rules for discussions, practice active listening and empathy, and encourage your team to communicate with you openly and honestly.

Using Technology to Enhance Communication

Building a Strong Team
Clear and effective communication is essential for building a strong team. In today's digital age, there are many ways

to stay connected with team members, regardless of location or time zones. Entrepreneurs should utilize technology to enhance communication and collaboration among team members.

First, entrepreneurs can use video conferencing tools such as Zoom or Skype to conduct virtual meetings. This is particularly useful when team members are working remotely or based in different locations. Video conferencing allows for face-to-face communication, which can help build stronger relationships and trust among team members.

Second, entrepreneurs can use messaging apps such as Slack or Microsoft Teams to facilitate real-time communication among team members. These apps allow team members to chat with one another, share files, and collaborate on projects.

Third, project management software such as Asana or Trello can be used to assign tasks, set deadlines, and track progress. This can help team members stay organized and focused on their goals.

However, while technology can enhance communication, it's important to remember that it's not a substitute for face-to-face interaction. Entrepreneurs should aim to balance digital communication with in-person meetings or team-building activities whenever possible.

Using technology to enhance communication can help entrepreneurs build a strong and cohesive team, regardless of location or time zones. However, it's important to strike a balance between digital communication and face-to-face interaction to ensure that team members feel connected and engaged.

Creating a Positive and Supportive Environment for Communication

Chapter 6

Creating a Positive and Supportive Environment for Communication

Communication is the key to building a strong team. In order to ensure that your team works cohesively and effectively, it is crucial to establish an environment where open communication is encouraged and valued. This involves creating a culture of trust and respect, where team members feel comfortable sharing their thoughts and ideas.

To create a positive and supportive environment for communication, you should start by setting clear expectations. This involves defining the role of communication in your organization, and outlining the standards for how communication should take place. You should also ensure that all team members are aware of the importance of communication, and how it contributes to the success of the business.

Another important aspect of creating a positive and supportive environment for communication is to provide regular feedback. This involves giving constructive feedback to team members on a regular basis, and acknowledging their strengths and weaknesses. This will help to build trust and encourage team members to communicate openly and honestly.

Effective communication also requires active listening. This means taking the time to listen to team members' thoughts and ideas, and asking follow-up questions to gain clarity. By actively listening, you show your team members that their opinions are valued, which will encourage them to communicate more freely.

In addition to these strategies, you can also create forums for open communication to take place. This could involve organizing regular team meetings, creating an online platform for discussion, or implementing a suggestion box for team members to provide anonymous feedback.

Ultimately, building a strong team requires effective communication skills. By creating a positive and supportive environment for communication, you can foster a culture of open communication where team members feel valued and empowered. This will help to ensure that your team works cohesively and effectively, leading to the success of your business.

Raising Capital and Managing Finances

Understanding Your Financial Needs

Assessing Financial Goals

As an entrepreneur, it's crucial to understand your financial goals and needs before raising capital or managing your finances. It's important to take stock of your current financial situation and map out a plan for reaching your desired financial outcomes. This requires you to assess your current financial status, determine your future financial goals, and identify potential obstacles that may stand in your way.

Assessing your financial goals involves taking a holistic view of your financial situation. This includes assessing your income, expenses, assets, and liabilities. It's important to have a solid understanding of your current cash flow, debt-to-income ratio and net worth. By taking these factors into account, you'll be able to determine your current financial situation and identify areas in which you might need to adjust your strategy.

Once you have a clear understanding of your current financial situation, it's time to determine your future financial goals. Ask yourself what kind of financial returns are you hoping to achieve from your entrepreneurial endeavors? Are you looking to generate a steady stream of income, build long-term wealth, or simply break even? Setting clear and specific financial goals will help guide your capital raising and financial management strategies.

Finally, it's important to take a close look at the potential obstacles that may stand in the way of achieving your financial goals. This may include market volatility, increased competition, or unexpected expenses. Identifying potential challenges upfront will allow you to plan proactively for events that may impact your financial outcomes.

By assessing your current financial goals, determining your future financial objectives, and identifying potential obstacles, you'll be better equipped to raise capital and manage your finances effectively. This will enable you to build a successful and sustainable business while minimizing financial risk.

Estimating Financial Requirements

Before you can adequately raise capital or manage your finances, it's important to understand your financial needs. This requires estimating how much money you will need to start and operate your business.

To do this, you must perform a thorough analysis of your business plan, taking into account all of the expenses associated with starting and running a company. This includes costs like rent, utilities, equipment, marketing, legal fees, and payroll, among others.

One approach is to break down your financial needs into two categories: fixed and variable costs. Fixed costs are expenses that remain the same, regardless of how much you sell or produce, such as rent. On the other hand, variable costs are dependent on production or sales volume, like raw materials.

Once you have identified all of the costs involved, it's time to create a cash flow projection. This will help you estimate how much money you'll need on a month-to-month basis, taking into account income and expenses. It's important to account for potential delays or setbacks that may occur during the early stages of the business.

With a clear understanding of what your financial requirements are, you'll be better equipped to raise capital and manage your finances effectively. It's always best to err on the side of caution and overestimate your financial needs, rather than underestimating and running into financial challenges down the line.

Identifying Funding Sources

Before diving into the world of fundraising, it's essential to understand the different types of financing available for startups. You must have a clear idea of the amount of money you need, what you need it for, and when you need it.

One of the most common funding sources among entrepreneurs is self-funding, where you invest your savings to bootstrap your business. However, this route may not be easy for everyone, and you may want to explore other sources.

Crowdfunding has become a popular funding option in recent years, where entrepreneurs can pitch their ideas to a broader audience and raise money from multiple investors.

It works well for products or services that can attract mass appeal and have a widespread target market.

Another option is equity financing, where you sell a portion of your business ownership in exchange for capital. This is suitable for startups with high-growth potential and can access angel investors or venture capitalists.

Finally, there are several grants and loans available exclusively for startups that cater to specific niches or industries. It's worth exploring these opportunities to secure non-dilutive funding and have an advantage in your early stages.

Identifying the right funding sources for your business requires a thorough analysis of your needs, available options, and their requirements. Once you've identified potential investors or lenders, you must have a compelling pitch and business plan to attract their attention and secure funding. The next section will cover the basics of pitching and raising capital.

Evaluating Short-term and Long-term Financing Options

As an entrepreneur, it is essential to understand your financial needs and the different financing options available to you. Evaluating both short-term and long-term financing options is crucial in determining what is best for your business.

Short-term financing options include lines of credit, credit cards, and trade credit. These options are ideal for meeting immediate financial needs like covering expenses, paying suppliers or purchasing inventory. While these options may be readily available, they often come with high-interest rates, which can be costly in the long run.

Long-term financing options include business loans, equipment loans, and commercial mortgages. These options are designed for larger expenses like purchasing property, buying expensive equipment, or expanding your business. However, securing long-term financing can be challenging and often require collateral like property or equipment.

It's essential to evaluate both short-term and long-term financing options carefully. Short-term financing can help you address the immediate needs of your business, but it may come with a high-interest rate, putting your business at risk in the long run. Long-term financing may provide more stability, but it requires significant financial planning and persistence since securing these loans can be challenging.

Understanding your financial needs is critical in determining the financing that suits your business best. Entrepreneurs must evaluate both short-term and long-term financing options to ensure they make the best decision for their business.

Preparing a Financial Plan

As an entrepreneur, it's crucial to understand your financial needs and prepare a comprehensive financial plan before launching your business. A financial plan is a document that outlines your projected income and expenses, identifies potential risks and opportunities, and establishes financial goals for your business.

To prepare a sound financial plan, you need to start by creating a cash flow forecast. A cash flow forecast is a statement that shows the inflows and outflows of cash over a specific period, usually a year. It helps you to understand your cash position and identify any potential cash flow problems.

The next step is to prepare a profit and loss statement (P&L). A P&L statement summarizes your revenues, costs, and expenses over a specific period, usually a year, to determine the profitability of your business. By analyzing your P&L statement, you can identify areas that need improvement and make informed decisions about pricing, marketing, and expenses.

Lastly, it's essential to create a balance sheet. A balance sheet summarizes your assets, liabilities, and equity at a specific point in time. It helps you to measure your business's financial health and determine its solvency and liquidity.

Preparing a financial plan is a critical step in managing your finances and raising capital for your business. It helps you to understand your financial needs, identify potential risks and opportunities, and establish financial goals. By creating a cash flow forecast, profit and loss statement, and balance sheet, you can make informed decisions and take control of your finances.

Raising Capital

Bootstrapping: Self-funding Your Business

In this subsection, we'll explore bootstrapping, which refers to starting and growing your business through self-funding. As an entrepreneur, you can use your own savings, personal credit cards or lines of credit, or even sell some possessions to raise the funds you need to get your business off the ground.

One advantage of bootstrapping is that you aren't dependent on external investors to provide seed money for your business. This means that you retain control over the equity and decision-making within your company. Plus, the more you invest in your business, the more confident potential investors may be in your venture since they can see your personal commitment to its success.

However, self-funding your business isn't without risks. You may need to invest a significant amount of your own resources, which could put a strain on your personal finances. Additionally, you may not have access to the same amount of capital as external investors, which could limit the growth potential of your business.

To mitigate these concerns, consider taking advantage of cost-saving measures, like working from home or using open-source software. This can help stretch your funds and make your business more efficient. Additionally, consider setting clear financial goals and developing a budget to ensure you are using your resources effectively.

Finally, don't forget to explore alternative funding options like crowdfunding or small business loans. These can provide additional capital to help your business grow while still allowing you to retain control. With careful planning and a willingness to take calculated risks, you can successfully bootstrap your business and build it up from the ground up.

Debt Financing: Borrowing Money from Investors

Raising Capital: Debt Financing - Borrowing Money from Investors

In this subsection, we will discuss one of the most common ways for entrepreneurs to raise capital: borrowing from investors. This involves seeking funds from individuals or institutions who are willing to lend money to your business in exchange for a promise of repayment with interest.

When seeking funds from investors, it is crucial to have a well-developed business plan that outlines your financial needs, proposed use of funds, projected returns, and risks associated with your venture. With this in hand, you can approach investors with the confidence that comes from being well-prepared.

There are several types of investors that you can approach for borrowing money, including banks, venture capitalists, angel investors, and friends and family. Each type of investor has its own requirements and expectations, so it is important to research and understand their interests and investment criteria.

For debt financing, banks are often the first place

entrepreneurs turn to for financing. However, it can be difficult for startups to get approved for traditional bank loans without substantial collateral or a proven track record of generating revenue.

Venture capitalists and angel investors are alternative options for businesses seeking large-scale funding. These investors typically provide funds in exchange for equity in the company, but they also tend to be more selective and involved in the decision-making process. This can be an advantage for companies that can benefit from strategic guidance, networking opportunities, and industry expertise.

Finally, seeking investment from friends and family can seem like a straightforward solution, but it is important to remember that this approach can come with emotional and financial risks. It is crucial to enter into these types of agreements with clear expectations and formal agreements in place to avoid potential conflicts down the line.

Borrowing money from investors can be an effective way to raise capital for your business, but it requires careful planning and research. Understanding the requirements and expectations of different investors, as well as the risks and rewards associated with each option, can help you find the funding solution that is right for your business.

Equity Financing: Issuing Shares to Investors

Equity Financing: Issuing Shares to Investors

When a business needs funding, one option is to raise capital by issuing shares to investors. Equity financing allows a company to sell ownership stakes to individuals or organizations in exchange for investment. This approach can be attractive to investors who are looking for a stake in the company's success.

However, it's important to understand the implications of issuing shares. For one, the company will need to have a valuation and determine how many shares will be offered. Additionally, the ownership structure of the business will be impacted by the sale of shares.

Before embarking on an equity financing strategy, it's important to consider the benefits and drawbacks. On the positive side, this approach allows for a diverse range of investors who can provide financial backing, industry expertise, and other resources to help the business grow. However, an equity financing strategy also means giving up partial ownership of the business and having to share decision-making authority with others.

To successfully implement an equity financing strategy, entrepreneurs must first do their research and understand the different types of investors that can be targeted. This includes private investors, venture capitalists, and institutional investors. Each of these investor types has different expectations, both in terms of potential return on investment and involvement in the company's operations.

When seeking equity financing, businesses will also need to clearly articulate their business proposition, outlining how they plan to use the funds and what potential returns investors can expect. This requires a solid business plan, including a growth strategy, financial projections, and an understanding of market opportunity.

Equity financing can be a powerful tool for raising capital and growing a business. However, it's important for entrepreneurs to carefully evaluate the implications of issuing shares and to have a solid plan in place for executing this strategy. Ultimately, with the right mix of investment and expertise, equity financing can set a business on the path to success.

Crowdfunding: Campaigning Online to Raise Capital

Raising Capital and Managing Finances
Crowdfunding is a method of raising capital in which an entrepreneur seeks small contributions from many individuals or organizations to fund a project or business. There are three main types of crowdfunding: donation-based, reward-based, and equity-based.

Donation-based crowdfunding is when entrepreneurs seek donations from individuals who support their idea or product. In return, the entrepreneurs may offer rewards such as products or services.

Reward-based crowdfunding is similar to donation-based crowdfunding, but entrepreneurs offer a specific reward in return for the contribution. For example, an entrepreneur can offer pre-orders of their product or exclusive access to their services.

Equity-based crowdfunding involves selling shares of the business or offering a percentage of ownership in exchange for contributions. This method is suitable for entrepreneurs who want to raise a significant amount of money and are willing to give up some control of their business.

Crowdfunding campaigns are typically conducted online,

using platforms such as Kickstarter, Indiegogo or GoFundMe. Entrepreneurs must create a compelling pitch or video that explains the concept of the business and the benefits of contributing.

Crowdfunding is an effective way for entrepreneurs to raise capital and receive support from a large number of people. However, entrepreneurs must be prepared to put in the effort to create an effective campaign that captures the attention of potential contributors.

Government Grants and Loans

One potential source of funding for entrepreneurial ventures is through government grants and loans. These can come from federal, state, or local government programs, and can vary in availability and criteria eligibility depending on the region.

Government grants are funds awarded to businesses with no requirement of repayment. These can apply to specific industries, minorities or women-owned businesses, or for research and development purposes. Some examples of government grant programs include the Small Business Innovation Research (SBIR) and Small Business Technology Transfer (STTR) programs, which fund the development and commercialization of new technologies.

Government loans, on the other hand, do require repayment with interest. The most well-known government loan program is the Small Business Administration's (SBA) loan program, which provides low-interest loans to small businesses. The SBA also offers disaster loans for businesses affected by natural disasters.

While government funding can provide a valuable source of capital for entrepreneurs, it is important to note that the application process can be time-consuming and competitive. It is crucial to research and understand the eligibility requirements and application process before pursuing government funding. Additionally, entrepreneurs must be prepared to comply with any reporting or compliance regulations associated with government funding.

Government grants and loans can offer a viable option for raising capital for entrepreneurial ventures, but it is important to approach these programs strategically and with a strong understanding of the requirements and expectations involved.

Managing Finances

Establishing Financial Controls

As an entrepreneur, one of your primary responsibilities is to manage your finances effectively. While raising capital is essential, it is equally crucial to establish financial controls that can help you manage your finances efficiently. However, before you can establish financial controls, you need to understand your financial needs and goals.

Firstly, you need to identify your financial objectives, such as increasing revenue, reducing expenses, or improving profitability. Without clearly defining your financial goals, it can be challenging to develop a plan to manage your finances effectively.

Once you have identified your financial objectives, you need to focus on establishing financial controls. Financial controls are the policies and procedures you use to ensure that your financial transactions are accurate and reliable. There are three primary types of financial controls: administrative controls, operational controls, and accounting controls.

Administrative controls are the policies and procedures you use to manage financial operations, such as managing cash flow, setting budgets, and handling financial reporting. Operational controls are the policies and procedures you use to manage day-to-day business operations, such as inventory management and purchasing.

Accounting controls are the policies and procedures you use to track and record financial transactions accurately.

Accounting controls help you identify and correct errors or discrepancies in your financial records. Some of the common accounting controls include balancing your books regularly, reconciling bank statements, and ensuring that all payments are correctly invoiced.

Effective financial controls require a systematic approach that involves regularly monitoring and evaluating the effectiveness of your financial controls. You need to ensure that your financial controls are aligned with your business goals and objectives and that they are being implemented effectively.

The key to establishing effective financial controls is to start small and build over time. You can begin by identifying your most critical financial operations and focusing on developing controls for those areas. As your business grows and your financial needs change, you can adapt your financial controls to keep pace with your business's growth.

Establishing financial controls is an essential part of managing your finances effectively. As an entrepreneur, you need to focus on defining your financial objectives and then develop a plan to establish financial controls. Effective financial controls require a systematic and proactive approach that involves regularly monitoring and evaluating the effectiveness of your financial controls.

Developing a Budget System

One of the essential aspects of running a business is managing finances effectively. Without a proper budget, it becomes challenging to keep track of expenses and cash flow, leading to financial difficulties. Developing a budget system requires discipline and attention to detail. However, the benefits of implementing a budget system are worth the effort.

The first step in creating a budget system is to identify all your sources of income. This could include sales revenue, investments, loans or grants. Once you have gathered all the information, you can start to estimate your cash inflow.

The next stage is to identify all your expenses, including fixed expenses, variable expenses, and one-off expenses. Fixed expenses are payments that remain constant every month, such as rent or employee salaries. Variable expenses, such as electricity bills, tend to fluctuate, while one-off expenses include purchases for equipment or special projects.

After identifying expenses, it's necessary to calculate cash outflow. You should consider reviewing previous months to get a better understanding of how much money you spend in each area. A cash outflow analysis can help you prioritize your expenses and focus on the critical areas first.

Once you have worked out your income and expenses, you can determine your monthly net cash flow. This amount is a key metric to understand your business's financial position and provides valuable insights for future financial planning.

Creating a budget system involves regular monitoring and adjustments. It's necessary to keep track of all cash inflows and outflows and make changes as needed. This lets you modify expenses and expenditures to ensure you have enough cash to cover unexpected costs or invest in new opportunities.

A budget system provides a framework for managing your business finances, which can help avoid financial difficulties and improve your financial position. The process of developing and maintaining a budget requires discipline and attention to detail, but the benefits of a well-executed budget far outweigh the effort required to create it.

Creating Financial Statements

As a business owner, it's crucial to understand the financial health of your company. Creating financial statements is an effective way to track your business's financial progress.

There are three main types of financial statements: income statements, balance sheets, and cash flow statements. Each statement provides different insights and information about the company's financial performance.

The income statement shows the revenue and expenses of the company over a specific period. This statement is useful in determining if a company is profitable and how much profit it has made.

The balance sheet provides a snapshot of the company's financial position at a specific point in time. It shows the company's assets, liabilities, and equity. This statement is useful in determining the company's financial health and its ability to pay its debts.

The cash flow statement shows how much cash the company has generated and how much it has spent over a specific period. It provides insights into the company's cash flow, which is essential for its survival and growth.

It's crucial to ensure that your financial statements are accurate and up-to-date. This way, you can make informed decisions about your business's financial health and plan for the future. Hiring a professional accountant or investing in accounting software can help ensure the accuracy and quality of your financial statements.

Tracking Cash Flow

As an entrepreneur, it's essential to be able to manage your business finances effectively. One of the key components of financial management is tracking your cash flow.

Cash flow refers to the amount of money that goes in and out of your business over a specific period. To effectively manage your cash flow, you need to track all of your business's expenses, including overhead costs such as rent, utilities, and salaries, as well as costs of goods sold.

Tracking your cash flow enables you to identify any discrepancies in your expenses or delays in payments from customers. As such, it's essential to keep accurate and up-to-date records of all transactions to ensure that your business stays profitable.

Several tools can help you track your cash flow effectively. You can use spreadsheets or accounting software to organize and automate your financial tracking. Additionally, you should regularly review and analyze your cash flow statements to identify areas of improvement and take corrective action when necessary.

Maintaining a positive cash flow is crucial to the success of your business. With good financial management practices in place, you'll be able to ensure that your business always has enough resources to cover expenses, invest in growth opportunities, and achieve long-term success.

Monitoring Financial Performance

In order for your business to succeed, you must constantly be monitoring your financial performance. It's important to stay on top of your revenues, expenses, profits, and losses. This will help you make informed decisions and see where you can cut costs and increase profits.

One of the most important tools for monitoring financial performance is the income statement. This statement shows your revenues and expenses over a specific period of time. By analyzing your income statement, you can see where your money is coming from and where it's going.

Another important tool is the balance sheet. This statement shows your assets, liabilities, and equity at a specific point in time. By analyzing your balance sheet, you can see your company's financial health and how much debt you have.

Cash flow is also crucial to monitor, as it is the lifeblood of any business. You should always know how much cash you have on hand, how much you're bringing in, and how much you're spending. This will help you make important decisions about investments and expenses.

It's also important to have a budget in place. A budget will help you plan for the future by setting goals for revenue and expenses. You should compare your actual financial performance to your budget regularly to see if you're on track.

In addition to these tools, there are several financial ratios you can use to analyze your financial performance. These include the debt-to-equity ratio, the current ratio, and the gross profit margin. By analyzing these ratios, you can see how your company is performing in relation to its competitors and industry standards.

Monitoring your financial performance is essential for any business owner. By staying on top of your revenues, expenses, and profits, you can make informed decisions and keep your business on the road to success.

Implementing Effective Marketing Strategies

Building your brand

Creating a strong brand identity

Your brand identity is the face of your company. It's what people see and think of when they hear your company's name. Creating a strong brand identity is crucial for any business looking to succeed. Here are some key steps to follow while developing a strong brand identity:

Define Your Brand: Begin by defining what your brand stands for. Identify your brand values, mission statement, and unique selling proposition. This will help you establish a clear and compelling brand personality.

Identify Your Target Audience: Knowing your target audience is extremely important when developing your brand identity. You need to understand what they want, what they need, and what motivates them to purchase your products.

Create a Visual Identity: Your brand needs to have a visual identity that captures its values, personality, and key messaging. Design a logo and create a color scheme that resonates with your target audience.

Develop Brand Guidelines: Once you have established your brand identity, ensure it is consistent across all communication channels. Create brand guidelines that outline your brand's visual standards, messaging tone and style, and how it should be used on different mediums.

Consistently Communicate Your Brand: Be consistent with your messaging and visual communication across all channels. Use your brand identity in every piece of communication, from social media posts to product packaging. This will help build a strong and recognizable brand presence.

By following these key steps, you'll be well on your way to creating a strong brand identity for your company. Remember, your brand is your company's reputation, and a strong brand identity will help you establish and retain customer loyalty.

Understanding your target audience

Before you can begin to build your brand, you need to understand who your target audience is. Your target audience is the group of people who your product or service is designed for. Without a solid understanding of your target audience, it is impossible to create a brand that resonates with them.

To understand your target audience, you need to conduct market research. This research will help you identify important demographic information such as age, gender, income, education, and location. You will also want to understand the psychographics of your target audience, which includes their values, attitudes, and interests.

One effective way to conduct market research is through surveys. You can create an online survey using a platform like Google Forms or SurveyMonkey and distribute it to your target audience through social media or email. You can also conduct focus groups or interviews to gather more in-depth information.

Once you have a clear understanding of your target audience, you can begin to create a brand that will appeal to them. Your brand is more than just your logo and website design. It encompasses your company values, personality, and messaging. All of these elements must be carefully crafted to resonate with your target audience.

For example, if your target audience is environmentally conscious millennials, your brand should reflect your commitment to sustainability and social responsibility. Your messaging should emphasize the importance of protecting the planet and the role your company plays in that effort. You might also consider partnering with eco-friendly organizations or using sustainable materials in your packaging.

Understanding your target audience is a critical first step in building a strong brand. By conducting market research and creating a brand that resonates with your target audience, you can differentiate yourself from competitors and attract loyal customers.

Crafting a compelling brand message

Crafting a compelling brand message is crucial to standing out in a crowded marketplace. It sets the tone for how your business is perceived and helps to differentiate it from your competitors.

First, you need to define your brand personality. Is your brand playful or serious, innovative or traditional? This personality should align with your target audience's values and expectations, and it should be consistent across all messaging.

Next, focus on identifying your Unique Value Proposition (UVP). This is the unique benefit you offer that sets you apart from other businesses in your industry. Your UVP should be clear, concise, and benefit-focused. It should solve a problem or meet a need for your target audience.

Once you have a clear understanding of your brand personality and UVP, you can begin crafting your brand message. This message should convey your brand personality and UVP in a way that resonates with your target audience.

To do this effectively, use simple, clear language that your audience can easily understand. Avoid industry jargon or complex terms that may confuse or alienate potential customers. Focus on creating a message that is emotionally compelling and speaks to your target audience's pain points.

Finally, ensure that your brand message is consistent across all channels, from social media to advertising to packaging. This consistency builds trust and helps to reinforce your brand in the minds of your target audience.

Crafting a compelling brand message takes time and effort, but it is an essential component of building a successful business. By defining your brand personality, identifying your UVP, and crafting a clear and emotionally compelling message, you can differentiate your business and stand out in a crowded marketplace.

Building brand awareness

Implementing Effective Marketing Strategies: Building Your Brand

Building brand awareness is the first step towards establishing a recognizable and trusted brand. In today's digital age, it is essential to be actively present across various channels to connect with the target audience. Branding is all about creating a unique visual identity and message that resonates with the audience. Here are some ways to build brand awareness:

Creating a strong visual identity - A brand's visual elements, such as its logo, color palette, typography, and imagery, should reflect its values and mission. A well-designed logo can create a lasting impression and make the brand memorable.

Developing a consistent brand message - A strong brand message resonates with the audience and communicates your unique value proposition. A consistent message across all channels can create a unified brand image.

Leveraging influencer marketing - Collaborating with influencers can help reach a wider audience and build brand awareness. Influencers who align with the brand's values can endorse and promote the brand on their platforms.

Participating in community events - Participating in local events can help build relationships with the target audience and create brand awareness. Sponsoring events or hosting brand-related events can create a positive brand image.

Investing in paid advertising - Paid advertising on social media platforms and search engines can help reach the target audience and create brand awareness. Targeted ads can help reach the right audience and create brand awareness.

Building brand awareness is a continuous process, and brands need to remain relevant and adaptable to stand out in the market. By creating a strong visual identity, developing a consistent message, leveraging influencers, participating in community events, and investing in paid advertising, brands can reach a wider audience and build trust within the industry.

Developing brand loyalty

Developing brand loyalty is the key to long-term success in any business. It involves creating a positive image for your brand and developing a relationship with your customers that makes them want to come back again and again. Here are some tips on how to build brand loyalty:

Deliver on promises: One of the most important aspects of building brand loyalty is keeping your promises. If you promise your customers an exceptional product or service, you must deliver on that promise consistently.

Create a positive experience: People remember positive experiences more than negative ones. Make sure your customers have a positive experience every time they interact with your brand. Whether it's through your website, customer service, or in-store experience, make sure everything is top-notch.

Build a community: Your customers want to feel like they belong to something. By building a community, you can create a sense of belonging and loyalty. This can be done through social media groups, events or even special promotions for your most loyal customers.

Offer incentives: Offering incentives is a great way to build brand loyalty. Whether it's through a rewards program or exclusive discounts, make sure your customers feel appreciated for their loyalty.

Be consistent: Consistency is key to building brand loyalty. From your messaging to your visual identity, make sure everything is consistent throughout all channels.

By following these tips, you can build a strong foundation for brand loyalty and create long-lasting relationships with your customers. Remember, developing brand loyalty takes time and effort, but it's well worth it in the end.

Developing a content strategy

Creating valuable content

One of the most essential components of creating an effective content strategy is developing valuable content. Content that is valuable is not only informative but also engaging for your target audience. Valuable content addresses the pain points or solves the problems of your target audience.

When you are creating content, focus on providing value for your audience. One great way to create valuable content is to leverage the power of storytelling. Share personal anecdotes and experiences that your target audience can identify with. This will not only help to keep your audience engaged but also builds a connection with them.

Your content should also be informative and educational for your audience. Share your expertise or knowledge on your business or industry with your audience. This establishes you as a thought leader in your industry, making you an authority in your niche.

When creating valuable content, you have to consider the format that would be best suited for your target audience. This could be in the form of blog posts, videos, podcasts, webinars, infographics or e-books- the list goes on. Choose the format that your audience prefers and consistently deliver content in this format.

Creating valuable content requires time and effort, but it will pay off in the long run. The more value you provide your audience, the more they will trust and engage with your brand. By consistently creating valuable content, you build a loyal audience that will eventually become your brand ambassadors.

Choosing the right content platforms

Once you have identified your target audience and what type of content will resonate with them, it's time to determine which platforms to use for your content. Depending on your audience, some platforms may be more effective than others. Here are some considerations to keep in mind when choosing the right content platforms for your business:

Website/Blog:
A website or blog is a great place to house your content and act as a hub for your audience. It's also a great way to improve your SEO (Search Engine Optimization) and increase your visibility on search engines. Make sure your website is user-friendly, mobile responsive, and easy to navigate.

Social Media:
Social media is a powerful tool where you can connect with your audience and promote your content. With so many social media platforms available, it's essential to choose the right ones for your business. Consider the demographics of your target audience and the type of content you want to share.

Video Platforms:
Video content is becoming more popular, and video platforms like YouTube and Vimeo can be great places to reach your audience. If you're producing video content,

consider uploading it to these platforms and embedding it on your website or social media.

Email:
Email marketing is a powerful way to reach your audience directly. Consider creating a newsletter and sending it to your email list regularly. Make sure your emails are informative, engaging, and personalized.

Podcast:
Podcasting is becoming increasingly popular, and it can be an effective way to reach your audience. Try starting a podcast and sharing it on platforms like Apple Podcasts, Spotify, or Google Podcasts.

When choosing the right content platforms, it's essential to keep your audience in mind. Experiment with different platforms to see what works best for your business and audience. Don't be afraid to pivot if you're not seeing the results you want. The key is to be agile and adaptable as you grow your business.

Creating a content calendar

Creating a content calendar is an essential step in executing a successful content strategy. A content calendar is a schedule of content topics, types, and intended publication dates. It helps to plan and organize content creation in a structured manner to ensure that content is delivered consistently and regularly.

When creating a content calendar, it's important to consider the following factors:

Audience: Who is your target audience, and what content topics will they respond best to?

Channels: Which channels will you be publishing your content on?

Objectives: What are your content objectives? What do you want your audience to do after reading your content?

Themes: What broad themes will your content fall under?

Types of content: What types of content will you be publishing, such as blog posts, videos, or podcasts?

Once you have a clear understanding of the above factors, it's time to start creating your content calendar.

Here are the steps to creating a content calendar:

Determine how often you want to publish content.

Identify the themes for each month.

Determine the specific topics for each week.

Assign content types to each topic.

Set target publication dates for each piece of content.

Assign responsibilities to team members or freelancers if you have them.

Review and adjust the calendar periodically.

By creating a content calendar, you will be able to deliver a consistent stream of content to your audience, increase engagement, and build brand awareness.

Planning for content promotion

Content:

One of the crucial aspects of developing a successful content strategy is planning for content promotion. While it is essential to create high-quality content consistently, it would all be for nothing if no one sees it. Therefore, promoting your content effectively is critical to ensure that it reaches your target audience and generates the desired results.

The following are some key factors to consider when planning for content promotion:

Identify your target audience: To effectively promote your content, you need to know who your target audience is. Understanding their preferences, interests, and pain points is essential to tailor your content to their needs and create an emotional connection that motivates them to engage with your brand.

Determine the best distribution channels: After identifying your target audience, you need to determine the best channels to distribute your content. These could include social media platforms, email marketing, guest posting, influencer marketing, and paid advertising.

Develop a distribution plan: Once you have determined the best channels to distribute your content, you need to develop a plan that outlines the specific tactics and timelines for each channel. This plan should include details such as when to publish, the type of content to create, the frequency of distribution for each channel, and any other relevant details.

Measure and adjust: After implementing your promotion plan, it is important to measure the results to determine what is working and what needs to be adjusted. This could include analyzing engagement metrics such as views, shares, likes, comments, and conversions. Adjust your promotion plan accordingly based on the insights gained from your analysis.

Effective content promotion is a crucial component of a successful content strategy. By identifying your target audience, determining the best distribution channels, developing a detailed plan, and regularly measuring and adjusting your tactics, you can increase the visibility of your content and establish a strong online presence.

Measuring content performance

Developing a Content Strategy: Measuring Content Performance

Creating great content is an essential part of building a successful business, but creating high-quality content alone is not enough. As an entrepreneur, you need to ensure that your content performs well and achieves the desired results. In this subsection, we will cover how to measure the performance of your content and make data-driven decisions to improve its effectiveness.

There are a few metrics you need to pay attention to when measuring your content's performance:

Traffic: Traffic refers to the number of people who visit your website or blog to view your content. This number represents the potential audience for your content.
Engagement: Engagement refers to the number of people who interact with your content. This metric includes likes, shares, comments, and any other form of user engagement.
Conversions: Conversions refer to the number of people who take a specific action on your website, such as purchasing a product or subscribing to a newsletter.

To measure your content's performance, you will need to use analytics tools such as Google Analytics or social media analytics tools. These tools allow you to track the metrics mentioned above and gain insights into how your content is performing.

Here are some key steps you can take to measure your content's performance effectively:

Set up goals and track them: Before you start measuring your content's performance, make sure you have clear goals in mind. Are you looking to increase traffic, engagement, or conversions? Once your goals are set, use analytics tools to track your progress.
Analyze your data: Take a closer look at your data and analyze the trends. What types of content are performing well, and which ones are not? What topics are resonating with your audience? Identify what's working and what's not, and make data-driven decisions.
Continuously improve: Content marketing is an iterative process, so you need to continuously improve to stay relevant. Use the insights gained from your data analysis to improve your content's effectiveness.

By measuring your content's performance, you can identify

areas for improvement and optimize your content marketing strategy. It's essential to make data-driven decisions rather than relying on guesswork or assumptions. With the right approach, you can create content that resonates with your audience and drives business results.

Leveraging social media

Choosing the right social media platforms

In today's digital age, social media has become an essential tool for businesses to market themselves to their target audience. However, not all social media platforms are created equal, and not all of them are suitable for every business. That's why it's crucial to choose the right social media platforms to use as part of your marketing strategy.

Firstly, it's essential to understand your target audience and where they are most active. For instance, if your target audience is primarily young adults, you might want to focus on platforms like Snapchat, Instagram, and TikTok, which are popular among that demographic. On the other hand, if your target audience is older professionals, LinkedIn might be the way to go.

It's also important to consider the type of content you plan to create and share on social media. For instance, if you have a lot of high-quality visual content, platforms like Instagram or Pinterest might be more suitable. Conversely, if you plan to share long-form blog posts or articles, Facebook or LinkedIn may be the better choice.

Another crucial factor to consider is the amount of time and resources you have available to manage your social media presence. Trying to maintain an active presence on every social media platform can be overwhelming and time-consuming. Instead, it's better to focus on a few platforms where you can consistently create engaging content and interact with your audience.

Lastly, it's important to keep up with the latest trends and changes in social media. New platforms are emerging all the time, and existing ones are constantly evolving, so it's important to stay current and adapt your strategy accordingly.

Choosing the right social media platforms is crucial to the success of your marketing strategy. Consider your target audience, the type of content you plan to create and share, the resources you have available to manage your social media presence, and stay up-to-date with the latest trends and changes in the social media landscape.

Creating a social media strategy

Social media has paved the way for entrepreneurs to reach a broader audience and build their brand. It has also enabled them to engage with their customers in real-time, which is crucial for cultivating a loyal community. However, social media marketing requires a clear strategy to maximize its potential. Here's how you can create a social media strategy that works for your business:

Define your objectives: Before you begin your social media marketing efforts, it's crucial to identify your goals. These goals will serve as a guide to help you create a strategy that aligns with your overall business objectives. Your objectives could be to increase website traffic, generate leads, or build a strong brand reputation.

Know your audience: Understanding your target audience is essential to create content that resonates with them. It's crucial to look beyond demographics and delve deeper into their needs, preferences, and pain points. This information will help you tailor your content to meet their expectations and build a strong rapport with them.

Choose the right platforms: There are several social media platforms available, and each has a unique audience and purpose. It's important to select the platforms that align with your goals and audience. For instance, if you're targeting a younger audience, you might want to focus on platforms like Snapchat or TikTok, while LinkedIn is ideal for B2B businesses.

Develop a content strategy: A content strategy is a plan to create and distribute valuable content to your target audience. It should align with your objectives, audience, and the platforms you've chosen. Your content should be engaging, informative, and shareable. It should also be optimized for social media platforms by incorporating eye-catching visuals, hashtags, and keywords.

Monitor and measure your results: Finally, it's crucial to track and analyze your social media marketing efforts' effectiveness. This information will help you identify what's working and what's not so that you can refine your strategy accordingly. You can use tools like Google Analytics and social media analytics to track your metrics.

Creating a social media strategy requires a mix of creativity, research, and data analysis. By following these steps, you can develop a strategy that aligns with your business goals and helps you build a strong online presence.

Engaging with your audience on social media

Social media has become an integral part of our daily lives. It's where people connect, exchange, and stay informed about the latest happenings. The immense popularity of social media has opened up a world of opportunities for businesses to promote themselves and engage with their audience.

However, simply having a social media presence is not enough. The key lies in how you engage with your audience on social media. Here are some tips to help you make the most of your social media presence:

Respond Promptly: Social media is all about real-time interaction. Make sure to respond to your followers' comments, messages, and mentions promptly. Engage with them on a personal level, and show them that you value their feedback and opinions.

Use Visuals: Social media is a visual medium. Make sure to incorporate eye-catching visuals, such as images, videos, and infographics, into your social media posts. This will help you grab your audience's attention and convey your message effectively.

Keep it Genuine: Your social media presence should reflect your brand's personality and values. Always keep your communication genuine and authentic. Avoid using scripted responses or canned messages.

Offer Value: Your social media presence should go beyond self-promotion. Share valuable content with your audience, such as tips, insights, and industry news. This will help you establish your brand as a thought leader in your niche.

Be Consistent: Make sure to post regularly on your social

media profiles. This will help you stay top-of-mind with your audience and maintain engagement. Develop a content calendar and stick to it.

When done right, social media can be a powerful tool for businesses to build their brand, engage with their audience, and drive sales. By following these tips, you can develop a strong social media presence and make the most of the opportunities that social media has to offer.

Measuring the impact of social media

Social media has become an essential component of modern-day marketing strategies. It offers a plethora of opportunities for entrepreneurs to build their brand, connect with their target audience, and drive engagement. However, it is vital to evaluate the impact of your social media efforts to ensure your marketing strategies are continually evolving and improving.

There are several ways to measure the impact of social media. One way is to track engagement metrics, such as likes, comments, and shares. These metrics provide insights into the level of engagement your content is generating and how it compares to previous posts. By analyzing this data, you can identify the type of content that resonates most with your audience and refine your content strategy accordingly.

Another way to measure the impact of social media is to track website traffic. You can use a tool like Google Analytics to monitor the amount of traffic your website is receiving from social media platforms. By analyzing this data, you can determine which social media platforms are driving the most traffic to your website and adjust your social media strategies accordingly.

Conversion rates are another critical metric to track. A conversion rate is the percentage of website visitors who take a desired action after clicking on a link from social media. This action could be making a purchase, filling out a contact form, or subscribing to a newsletter. By monitoring conversion rates, you can identify which social media campaigns are working and adjust your strategies accordingly.

Customer feedback is also a valuable tool for measuring the impact of social media. Social media platforms provide a powerful communication channel between businesses and their customers. By engaging with your audience and encouraging them to leave feedback, you can gain valuable insights into the effectiveness of your social media strategies.

Measuring the impact of social media is critical to the success of your marketing strategies. By tracking engagement metrics, website traffic, conversion rates, and customer feedback, you can continually refine and improve your social media strategies to maximize their impact on your business.

Scaling your social media efforts

Social media platforms have become one of the most essential marketing channels for businesses today. They offer various opportunities to connect with potential customers, build brand awareness, and expand your reach. However, as your business grows, it's vital to scale your social media efforts to stay relevant and maintain your audience. Here are some practical ways to scale your social media efforts.

Plan a social media content calendar: As your business grows, you may need to increase the frequency, tone, and voice of your social media posts. Planning ahead is critical to keeping your audience engaged and your messaging consistent. Create a social media content calendar to schedule your social media posts more efficiently.

Invest in social media management tools: There are numerous social media management tools available that allow you to manage multiple social media accounts and streamline your social media marketing efforts. Some popular options include Hootsuite, Buffer, and Sprout Social.

Leverage user-generated content: Encourage your existing customers to create and share content that promotes your brand. User-generated content can result in new followers, increased engagement, and higher conversion rates. Share the user-generated content on your social media platforms to build trust, loyalty, and social proof.

Experiment with paid social media advertising: Social media advertising offers a highly targeted and cost-effective means to expand your social media reach. Platforms like Facebook, Instagram, and LinkedIn offer advanced targeting options based on demographic, interest, behavior, and location data.

Analyze and measure the effectiveness of your social media efforts: Metrics like engagement rates, reach, and conversion rates provide valuable insights into the success of your social media efforts. Use this data to optimize your social media content, refine your social media strategy, and continually improve your ROI.

Scaling your social media efforts can be a complex task, but it's an essential element of your marketing strategy. By planning ahead, leveraging user-generated content, investing in social media management tools, experimenting with paid advertising, and monitoring your metrics, you can maximize the impact of your social media efforts and achieve your marketing goals.

Overcoming Obstacles and Challenges

Mindset Shifts

Embracing Failure

For entrepreneurs, failure is not the end but a stepping stone to success. It is an opportunity to learn and grow, to identify what went wrong, and to pivot towards a better solution. Embracing failure as part of the journey is crucial to developing a resilient mindset, and understanding its role in the entrepreneurial process can help you overcome obstacles and challenges.

One of the key mindset shifts needed to embrace failure is reframing your perspective. Instead of seeing failure as a negative experience, try to see it as a learning opportunity. When you encounter a setback, take the time to reflect on what led to it, what could have been done differently, and how you can improve going forward.

Another way to embrace failure is to cultivate a growth mindset. This means adopting the belief that intelligence and abilities can be developed through hard work and dedication rather than being fixed traits. With a growth mindset, setbacks and failures are seen as challenges that can be overcome through effort and perseverance.

In addition to a growth mindset, having a strong sense of purpose and passion for your business can also help you embrace failure. When you are deeply committed to your vision, setbacks and failures become temporary roadblocks, rather than insurmountable barriers. By staying focused on your purpose and vision, you will be more resilient in the face of challenges and setbacks.

Ultimately, embracing failure is about shifting your mindset from a fixed, defeatist attitude to a growth-oriented, optimistic one. It takes practice and perseverance, but with time and effort, you can learn to see failures as opportunities for growth and progress. By embracing failure as an integral part of the entrepreneurial process, you can overcome obstacles and challenges and achieve success in your business.

Reframing Challenges as Opportunities

As an entrepreneur, you will face a variety of obstacles and challenges. These challenges can include financial struggles, lack of resources, competition, and personal setbacks. However, the way you approach these challenges can determine whether you succeed or fail. The most successful entrepreneurs have learned to reframe challenges as opportunities.

Reframing challenges means looking at setbacks as opportunities to learn and grow, rather than as roadblocks to success. It's all about changing your mindset from a negative to a positive perspective. Instead of feeling defeated, you can see each challenge as an opportunity to find new and innovative solutions.

For example, let's say you're struggling to find a way to increase sales. Instead of feeling defeated, you can reframe the challenge as an opportunity to connect with potential customers and learn what they're looking for in a product. This can lead to developing a new product or service that better meets the needs of your target audience.

Another example could be facing a lack of funding. Instead of giving up, you can reframe the challenge as an opportunity to get creative with your resources. Look for ways to cut costs or seek out alternative funding sources that you may not have considered before. This can lead to finding a way to grow your business with limited resources, which is a valuable skill for any entrepreneur.

In order to reframe challenges as opportunities, it's important to maintain a growth mindset. This means believing that you can improve your abilities and overcome obstacles through hard work and dedication. Practice resilience by viewing obstacles as opportunities to learn and adapt. Over time, this mindset shift can help you overcome even the most difficult challenges and lead to long-term success.

Persistence and Resilience

In the world of entrepreneurship, obstacles and challenges are inevitable. However, successful entrepreneurs understand that setbacks are just temporary roadblocks that can be overcome with persistence and resilience. In this subsection, we will explore the importance of cultivating a mindset of unwavering determination and the strategies that can help you bounce back from failures.

First and foremost, it's important to realize that persistence is not stubbornness. Stubbornness involves holding onto a particular strategy or approach despite clear evidence that it's not working. Persistence, on the other hand, involves recognizing when it's time to pivot or adjust course, but continuing to pursue your ultimate goals nonetheless.

One strategy for developing persistence is to focus on your "why." When you have a clear understanding of why you started your business in the first place and the impact that you want to make in the world, it becomes easier to stay motivated and persevere through tough times.

Another important mindset shift is the ability to bounce back from failures. Instead of seeing failures as indicators of your own limitations or worth, successful entrepreneurs view them as opportunities to learn and grow. They turn failures into productive learning experiences that can help them refine their strategies and make better decisions in the future.

In order to build resilience, it's important to practice self-care and cultivate healthy coping mechanisms. This might involve taking breaks when you're feeling overwhelmed, seeking support from friends and family members, or engaging in activities that help you unwind and recharge.

Above all, remember that perseverance and resilience are not innate traits that you either have or don't have. They are skills that can be learned and developed over time with practice and commitment. As you face challenges and obstacles in your entrepreneurial journey, remember that setbacks are not failures, and that with persistence and resilience, you can achieve your goals and make a positive impact in the world.

Growth Mindset

When facing obstacles and challenges, it is important for entrepreneurs to adopt a growth mindset. This mindset allows for the belief that challenges are opportunities to learn and develop new skills, rather than roadblocks to success. By embracing a growth mindset, entrepreneurs can shift their focus from the fear of failure and the limitations of their current circumstances, to the possibilities of growth and development.

One practical way to develop a growth mindset is to cultivate a sense of curiosity and a willingness to learn from setbacks. This can involve reframing negative experiences as opportunities for growth, asking for feedback from colleagues and mentors, and actively seeking out new skills and knowledge to improve one's business.

Another aspect of adopting a growth mindset is the ability to view failure as a natural part of the learning process. Rather than being discouraged by setbacks, entrepreneurs with a growth mindset understand that failure is an opportunity to refine their approach and make improvements. They also recognize that success is not a linear process, and that setbacks and challenges are often necessary steps on the path to achieving their goals.

Finally, entrepreneurs with a growth mindset prioritize continual improvement and are willing to put in the hard work required to achieve success. They understand that growth and development require dedication, persistence, and a willingness to take risks and step outside one's comfort zone.

By embracing a growth mindset, entrepreneurs can overcome obstacles and challenges with resilience and determination, and achieve their goals through a mindset of continual learning and development.

Entrepreneurial Thinking

Entrepreneurial thinking is a critical component of the entrepreneurial mindset. It involves seeing possibilities and opportunities where others may see only obstacles and difficulties. Entrepreneurial thinking is all about taking calculated risks and stepping outside of one's comfort zone. It is about being proactive, persistent, and driven to succeed.

In order to develop an entrepreneurial mindset, it is important to adopt a growth mindset. This means embracing challenges, learning from failures and setbacks, and taking action in the face of uncertainty. Adopting a growth mindset enables entrepreneurs to see challenges as opportunities for growth and improvement, rather than as roadblocks to success.

Another key aspect of entrepreneurial thinking is having a laser focus on one's goals and vision. Successful entrepreneurs remain focused on their ultimate objective while being flexible in their approach. They are constantly adapting to changing circumstances and making adjustments as necessary. In order to do this effectively, entrepreneurs must be able to think critically and creatively, and be willing to take risks.

Finally, entrepreneurial thinking involves having a mindset of abundance rather than scarcity. Rather than thinking in terms of limitations and scarcity, successful entrepreneurs focus on abundance and growth. This means cultivating a mindset of possibility, creativity, and optimism, and constantly seeking out new opportunities for growth and expansion.

Developing an entrepreneurial mindset involves adopting a growth mindset, remaining focused on goals and vision, thinking critically and creatively, and cultivating a mindset of abundance. By adopting these mindsets, entrepreneurs are better equipped to overcome obstacles and challenges, and to succeed in the long term.

Strategies

Problem-Solving Techniques

As an entrepreneur, you will encounter various obstacles and challenges along the way. Some obstacles may include financial difficulties, market competition, technological advancements, and more. However, the ability to overcome such challenges is essential to the success of your business.

To overcome obstacles effectively, you must employ problem-solving techniques that can help you identify the root of the problem and implement actionable solutions. One of the most useful problem-solving techniques is the 5 Whys Method. This technique involves asking a series of "why" questions to get to the root cause of the problem. For instance, if your business is experiencing a decline in sales, you could start asking, "Why are sales declining?" and keep asking "why" until you uncover the underlying issue.

Another effective technique is brainstorming. It involves gathering individuals or team members to generate ideas and possible solutions. It's an excellent approach to help you develop new perspectives and ideas outside of your traditional methods. You can also try mind mapping, which is a graphical technique designed to help you organize your thoughts and ideas through a visual representation of concepts, ideas, and relationships.

Furthermore, effective communication is essential in any problem-solving process. As a business owner, you need to communicate effectively with team members, stakeholders, and customers to gather and understand relevant information. You should also communicate the problem-solving process and progress to ensure everyone is on the same page.

Finally, you must be willing to take risks and be flexible in your approach to problem-solving. Taking risks means that you are willing to try new things, evaluate their results, and iterate to improve outcomes continually. Being flexible, on the other hand, will help you adapt to unexpected changes and challenges, effectively pivoting your business model whenever necessary.

By employing these problem-solving techniques, communication strategies, risk-taking, and flexibility, you will be better equipped to overcome challenges and obstacles that threaten your business's success.

Time Management

Effective time management skills are essential in the life of an entrepreneur. Entrepreneurs have multiple responsibilities that demand their time and attention, from meeting with clients, managing team members, and completing business-related tasks. In order to maintain a work-life balance and meet deadlines, it is crucial for entrepreneurs to manage their time effectively.

One way to manage time effectively is by prioritizing tasks. Entrepreneurs should create a to-do list of all the tasks that need to be completed and prioritize them based on their importance and urgency. This allows the entrepreneur to focus on the most important tasks and avoid wasting time on tasks that are not as critical.

Another effective time management strategy for

entrepreneurs is to delegate tasks to team members. Entrepreneurs should identify tasks that can be delegated to team members and provide them with clear instructions on how to complete them. This allows the entrepreneur to focus on tasks that require their expertise and knowledge, while team members complete tasks that can be done by others.

In addition, entrepreneurs should leverage technology to help manage their time. There are several productivity tools and software available that can help entrepreneurs streamline their work and save time. For instance, project management software can help keep track of deadlines and progress on various projects, while scheduling software can help manage appointments, meetings, and deadlines.

Lastly, entrepreneurs should ensure that they take breaks in between work, as this can help improve productivity and focus. Taking short breaks to do something relaxing can refresh the mind and help the entrepreneur approach tasks with renewed energy and focus.

By implementing effective time management strategies, entrepreneurs can overcome obstacles and challenges and work towards building a successful business.

Decision Making

As an entrepreneur, you will face countless decisions, both big and small, that will ultimately impact the success of your business. The ability to make effective decisions is critical to overcoming obstacles and staying on track towards your goals.

One effective strategy for decision making is to gather as much information as possible about the options at hand. This may involve research, seeking advice from experts or mentors, and considering the opinions of others on your team.

Another important strategy is to carefully weigh the potential risks and benefits of each option. It can be helpful to create a pros and cons list or use a decision-making matrix to objectively evaluate each option based on predetermined criteria.

Ultimately, the key to effective decision making is to understand your own values, goals, and priorities. By aligning each decision with these core beliefs, you can ensure that you are making choices that will lead you closer to achieving your vision for your business. It's also important to trust your instincts, take calculated risks, and be willing to adjust course when necessary.

Remember, the ability to make effective decisions is not something that comes naturally to everyone, but it can be developed and improved over time with practice and experience.

Resourcefulness

Resourcefulness is a critical attribute for any entrepreneur to possess. It refers to the ability to find creative solutions to problems, even when resources are limited. Resourcefulness is an essential skill because entrepreneurs often face unexpected problems that require quick and effective solutions.

The following strategies can help entrepreneurs become more resourceful.

Strategy 1: Keep an open mind

Successful entrepreneurs know that sometimes the best ideas come from unexpected sources. They keep an open mind and embrace opportunities to learn from others, whether it's through books, podcasts, or talking to experts in their field. By keeping an open mind, entrepreneurs can find creative solutions to problems that they may not have thought of otherwise.

Strategy 2: Learn to improvise

Entrepreneurs often face unexpected challenges that require them to think on their feet. Improvisation involves the ability to make quick decisions and adapt to changing circumstances. By learning to improvise, entrepreneurs can stay calm in the face of uncertainty and find creative solutions to problems.

Strategy 3: Embrace failure

Failure is a natural part of the entrepreneurial journey. Successful entrepreneurs know that they will face setbacks and failures along the way. Instead of viewing failure as a negative, entrepreneurs should embrace it as an opportunity to learn and grow. By embracing failure, entrepreneurs can become more resilient and better equipped to overcome obstacles.

Strategy 4: Build a network of support

Entrepreneurship can be a lonely journey, but it doesn't have to be. Building a network of support can help entrepreneurs stay motivated and overcome obstacles. This network can include mentors, peers, and even online communities.

Strategy 5: Focus on what you can control

Entrepreneurs face many variables that are outside of their control. By focusing on what they can control, entrepreneurs can maximize their chances of success. This strategy involves identifying the variables that are within their control and finding ways to optimize them.

Resourcefulness is a critical skill for entrepreneurs to possess. By keeping an open mind, learning to improvise, embracing failure, building a network of support, and focusing on what they can control, entrepreneurs can overcome obstacles and achieve success.

Adaptability

To be a successful entrepreneur, one must have adaptability as a core trait. Change is inevitable, and it is crucial to be ready to pivot when things don't go as planned. This skill is especially essential in today's fast-paced and ever-changing business landscape.

Adaptability requires being open-minded and not getting too attached to initial ideas or plans. Sometimes a radical shift in direction is necessary to stay relevant and competitive. Successful entrepreneurs not only embrace change but seek it out and use it to their advantage.

Here are some strategies for developing adaptability as an entrepreneur:

Embrace failure: Failure is unavoidable in entrepreneurship, and it's necessary to reframe it as a learning opportunity. Instead of wallowing in defeat, take the time to analyze what went wrong and pivot based on those findings.

Stay informed: Keep up to date with industry trends and developments. Being aware of shifts in your market and industry can help you anticipate necessary changes before they become emergencies.

Surround yourself with diverse perspectives: You don't know what you don't know, and that's why it's crucial to have diverse input. Surround yourself with people from different backgrounds and with different ways of thinking to encourage new ideas and identify blind spots.

Be open to feedback: Feedback is essential for growth, and being receptive to it will make you a better entrepreneur. Seek out input from mentors, advisors, and even customers, and use it to inform your decisions.

By developing adaptability as an entrepreneur, you'll be able to navigate change and overcome obstacles with greater ease. This skill will help you stay innovative, relevant, and competitive in today's ever-changing business landscape.

Support Systems

Mentors and Coaches

Entrepreneurship can be a daunting endeavor. It is filled with challenges, roadblocks, and setbacks. The key to overcoming these challenges is to have a strong support system in place. Many successful entrepreneurs credit their mentors and coaches with providing them with the guidance they needed to overcome the obstacles they faced.

Mentors can be anyone who has more experience or knowledge than you do in a particular area. They can help you navigate the challenges you encounter and provide guidance based on their own experiences. Coaches, on the other hand, are professionals who are trained to help you achieve your goals. They can help you identify your strengths and weaknesses, develop strategies for overcoming obstacles, and hold you accountable for taking action.

Finding the right mentor or coach can be a challenging task. You need to find someone who has experience in your industry or with the challenges you face. You also need to find someone who you trust and respect.

One way to find a mentor or coach is to attend networking events and industry conferences. This is a great way to meet people who have experience in your field and who may be willing to share their knowledge with you. You can also reach out to people in your network who you admire and ask them if they would be willing to mentor you or recommend a coach.

When working with a mentor or coach, it is important to be open and honest about your goals and challenges. This will help them provide you with the guidance you need. It is also important to be receptive to their feedback and willing to make changes based on their recommendations.

Having a mentor or coach can be a valuable asset when it comes to overcoming the obstacles and challenges of entrepreneurship. They can provide you with the guidance, support, and accountability you need to achieve your goals and succeed in your business.

Accountability Partners

Accountability Partners

As an entrepreneur, it can be challenging to stay on track and remain focused on your goals. This is where having an accountability partner can be extremely helpful.

An accountability partner is someone who you regularly check in with to discuss progress towards your goals. This could be a fellow entrepreneur, a mentor or a coach.

Having an accountability partner can provide numerous benefits. Firstly, it helps to keep you motivated and accountable for your actions. When you know that someone else is watching your progress, it's much harder to make excuses or give up when things get tough.

Furthermore, an accountability partner can offer valuable advice and feedback on your goals and progress. They can provide a different perspective and help you to overcome any challenges or obstacles that you may be facing.

When choosing an accountability partner, it's important to find someone who is supportive and committed to helping you achieve your goals. Ideally, they should have experience and expertise in your industry or area of focus.

To establish a successful accountability partnership, it's important to set clear goals and expectations upfront. Schedule regular check-ins and be honest and open about your progress and any challenges that you may be facing.

Remember, your accountability partner is not there to judge you or criticize your actions. They are there to support you and help you to achieve your goals. By working together, you'll be able to overcome any obstacles and create a successful and sustainable business.

Professional Networks

In addition to a strong mindset and effective strategies, successful entrepreneurs have a strong support system in place to overcome challenges and achieve their goals. One crucial aspect of this support system is professional networks, which can provide valuable resources, insights, and connections.

Building and maintaining professional networks is especially important for entrepreneurs, who often operate in highly competitive and fast-changing market environments. By staying connected with other business owners, industry experts, and potential partners or customers, entrepreneurs can stay ahead of the curve, identify new opportunities, and access critical resources when needed.

One effective way to build professional networks is to attend industry conferences, events, and networking groups. These venues provide opportunities to meet and connect with other professionals, learn about new trends and technologies, and share insights and best practices. Entrepreneurs can also join online groups and forums related to their industry or niche, participate in online discussions, and connect with other business owners on social media platforms.

While building professional networks is important, it's equally important to nurture and maintain these relationships over time. Entrepreneurs should make an effort to stay in touch with contacts, follow up after meetings and events, and offer value in return. By providing helpful resources, referrals, or expertise to their network, entrepreneurs can establish themselves as trusted and respected members of their community, while also reaping the benefits of a strong support system to help overcome obstacles and achieve their goals.

Emotional Support

In entrepreneurship, obstacles and challenges are inevitable. It's crucial to have strong support systems to navigate and overcome these hurdles. Emotional support is one vital aspect of such a system; it helps entrepreneurs maintain their mental and emotional wellbeing.

For starters, emotional support can come from friends and family members who provide a listening ear and a shoulder to lean on. Having a network of people who are supportive, understanding, and empathetic can be incredibly beneficial for an entrepreneur who is facing tough times.

In addition to family and friends, entrepreneurial peers are also an excellent source of emotional support. Others who have walked the same path and faced similar challenges can provide empathy, advice and offer practical solutions.

Working with a mentor or a coach is another way to receive emotional support. These individuals can be a sounding board for new ideas, as well as provide accountability and guidance. Entrepreneurs should seek out and foster relationships with mentors or coaches, as they can offer valuable insight and support in both good times and bad.

Finally, taking care of physical health can also support emotional wellbeing. Eating a balanced diet, getting enough exercise, and taking time to rest and recharge are all essential components of self-care. Ensuring that basic physical needs are met can help entrepreneurs feel better equipped to handle challenges and obstacles.

Having strong emotional support systems that include family, friends, peers, mentors, and self-care practices can be essential to an entrepreneur's success. It allows them to tackle obstacles with a clear and healthy mind and keeps them on a path to success.

Continuing Education

As an entrepreneur, it's crucial to stay up-to-date with the latest trends, technologies, and best practices in your field. One way to accomplish this is through continuing education.

Continuing education can take many forms, including

attending workshops, conferences, and seminars. These events provide an opportunity to learn from experts in your industry and to connect with other entrepreneurs facing similar challenges.

Another option is to enroll in online courses or programs. Many universities and educational institutions offer courses in entrepreneurship, business management, and related fields. These courses provide a structured learning environment and can be completed at your own pace.

It's also essential to keep up with industry publications and resources. Reading industry-specific blogs, websites, and forums can provide valuable insights into current trends and developments.

Finally, don't overlook the value of mentorship. Finding a mentor who has successfully navigated the challenges of entrepreneurship can provide invaluable guidance and support.

Continuing education is an ongoing process that requires a commitment to lifelong learning. By investing in yourself and staying up-to-date with the latest trends and best practices, you'll be better equipped to overcome obstacles and achieve success as an entrepreneur.

Putting it All Together: Applying the Entrepreneurial Mindset

Building a Personal Brand

Defining Your Unique Value Proposition

When it comes to building a personal brand, defining your unique value proposition is an essential step. This is what sets you apart from everyone else and communicates what you bring to the table. Your unique value proposition should be easy to understand, captivating, and demonstrate how you can solve your customer's problem.

To define your unique value proposition, start by identifying what sets you apart from others. This could be a unique skillset, experience, or approach to business. Consider what your customers or clients value most about your products, services, or experiences. Use this information to craft a proposition that is appealing to your target market.

Once you have defined your unique value proposition, make sure to communicate it clearly and consistently across all of your marketing channels. Your website, social media, and advertising should all reinforce this message. Keep in mind that your unique value proposition should align with your brand messaging and business goals.

Your unique value proposition is not a one-time thing. You

may need to tweak it as your business grows and evolves, or as your target market changes. Continuously evaluate your proposition to ensure it remains relevant and compelling to your audience.

Defining your unique value proposition is crucial to building a strong personal brand. It helps communicate what sets you apart from others and how you can offer value to your customers or clients. Make sure to communicate this message consistently across all of your marketing channels and evaluate it regularly to ensure it remains compelling to your audience.

Creating a Consistent Brand Identity

As an entrepreneur, building a personal brand is essential for creating a lasting impact on your clients and customers. A brand identity is the way you present yourself and your business, and it should be consistent throughout all your marketing efforts.

To create a consistent brand identity, you must start with a clear understanding of your brand's message and values. What are you trying to convey to your audience? What sets you apart from your competitors? Knowing your brand's unique selling points and your target audience will help you build a clear and consistent message.

Once you have a clear understanding of your brand, it's time to create a visual representation of your brand's identity. This includes your company logo, color scheme, font, and imagery. Your brand's visual identity should be consistent across all marketing channels, from your website to social media profiles and business cards.

Another important aspect of creating a consistent brand identity is using consistent language and tone in all communication with your clients and customers. This includes email, website copy, social media posts, and any other communication channels you use. Consistency in your messaging helps build trust and reinforces your brand's identity.

It's also essential to monitor your brand's reputation online and respond to any negative feedback promptly. Your online presence and customer reviews impact your brand's image, so it's crucial to keep a close eye on your reputation and address any issues that arise promptly.

Building a consistent brand identity is about understanding your brand's message and values, creating a visual representation of your brand's identity, using consistent language and tone in all communication, and monitoring your brand's online reputation. By doing so, you can build a strong and lasting brand that resonates with your audience and sets you apart from your competitors.

Developing a Brand Story

As an entrepreneur, one of the most important tasks you have is to ensure that your personal brand accurately represents who you are, what you stand for, and what you can offer to your customers or clients. Developing a brand story is a crucial step in building a strong personal brand that can stand the test of time.

The first step in developing a brand story is to identify the key elements that make you and your business stand out.

This could be your unique skills, experiences, or passions that set you apart from the competition. Once you have identified these key elements, you can start to weave them together into a cohesive narrative that tells your story in a compelling way.

Your brand story should be authentic and honest, and it should resonate with your target audience. It should also be consistent across all of your marketing and branding efforts, from your website and social media profiles to your business cards and promotional materials.

To develop your brand story, start by answering some key questions about yourself and your business. Who are you? What are your core values? What inspired you to start your business, and what do you hope to achieve? What unique skills, experiences, or perspectives do you bring to the table? Once you have answered these questions, you can start to craft a narrative that speaks to your target audience and highlights the key attributes that make you and your business unique.

Keep in mind that your brand story should be flexible and adaptable as your business grows and evolves. You should regularly revisit and update your brand story to ensure that it accurately reflects who you are and what you have to offer. By developing a strong brand story, you can build an authentic and compelling personal brand that sets you apart from the competition and helps you achieve your business goals.

Building an Authentic Online Presence

In today's digital age, having a strong and authentic online presence is essential for any entrepreneur looking to establish a personal brand. Your online presence is how you are seen, known, and perceived by your audience. Therefore, it is vital to present a true reflection of yourself and your values in all your online activities.

To build an authentic online presence, you need to:

Define your niche: It's essential to identify your niche and target audience first. This will help you tailor your content, messaging and storytelling to suit your audience's needs and preferences.

Develop your brand voice: Your brand voice is the tone and style in which you communicate with your audience. It should be consistent, conversational and unique to you. Pat Flynn's brand voice is friendly and conversational, which has helped him build a loyal following.

Create valuable content: Your content should provide value and help solve your audience's problems. It should align with your brand's values and be informative, engaging, and shareable.

Use social media strategically: Social media is an essential tool for building a personal brand. Choose the platforms that align with your niche and target audience, and use them consistently to share your content, engage with your audience and build relationships.

Be authentic and transparent: In today's world, people value authenticity and transparency. Be true to yourself and your values, and share your successes and failures with your audience. This creates a deeper connection and builds trust with your audience.

Building an authentic online presence is crucial for any entrepreneur looking to establish a personal brand. By defining your niche, developing your brand voice, creating valuable content, using social media strategically, and being authentic and transparent, you can build a strong online brand that resonates with your audience and helps you achieve your business goals.

Nurturing Your Network

Your network can play a significant role in building your personal brand. Nurturing your network by maintaining relationships and creating new connections can provide a wealth of opportunities. It is essential to be intentional about how you engage with your network and show genuine interest in their lives and professional endeavors.

One way to nurture your network is to consistently provide value through your interactions. Share relevant industry news, connect them with people who can help with their businesses, and offer your expertise when appropriate. Staying top of mind with your network means that they are more likely to think of you when opportunities arise.

Another important aspect of networking is attending events where you can meet new people and expand your network. Look for events related to your industry or interests and approach these events with a curious mindset. Focus on building genuine connections rather than just collecting business cards. Research attendees beforehand and prepare thoughtful questions that show your interest in their work.

Finally, don't forget to maintain your current relationships. Schedule regular check-ins with those in your network to catch up on their latest ventures and updates. Use these conversations to find opportunities to collaborate or offer support.

By nurturing your network, you can build a personal brand that is both influential and organic. Your network will become ambassadors for your brand and help you expand your reach within your industry.

Maximizing Your Business Potential

Setting SMART Goals

Once you have a vision for your business, the next step is to establish the specific goals that will help you achieve it. Goals that are poorly defined, unrealistic, or that lack relevance to your overall vision can become unattainable or even counterproductive.

One approach to creating useful goals is the SMART methodology. SMART stands for Specific, Measurable, Achievable, Relevant, and Time-bound. This approach ensures that each goal is well-defined, attainable, and has a clear deadline.

Specific: Goals should be clear and precise. For example, instead of a vague goal of "increasing revenue," a more specific goal would be "increasing revenue by 10% by the end of the year."

Measurable: Goals should be quantifiable so that you can track your progress. "10% increase in revenue" is measurable, while "increasing revenue" is not.

Achievable: Goals should be realistic and attainable. While it's good to be ambitious, it's not productive to set goals that are impossible to achieve with your resources.

Relevant: Goals should align with your overall business strategy and vision. Pursuing a goal that doesn't align with your vision can lead to wasted resources and lost time.

Time-bound: Goals should have a set deadline so that

progress can be tracked and adjustments can be made. Setting a specific date provides an added level of accountability.

Using the SMART framework, you can create goals that are specific, measurable, achievable, relevant, and time-bound. By establishing these goals, you can measure your progress and make adjustments when necessary to stay on track towards your vision.

Evaluating Your Business Model

To maximize your business potential, you need to have a clear understanding of your business model. Your business model is the foundation of your company, and it determines your success or failure. Therefore, you need to evaluate your business model regularly to ensure it is up to date and is still relevant in the current market.

The first step in evaluating your business model is to identify the key components. This includes your value proposition, target market, distribution channels, revenue streams, and cost structure. Once you have identified these components, you need to analyze them individually and as a whole to determine how they are contributing to your overall success.

When analyzing your value proposition, ask yourself if it is still relevant and valuable to your target market. Are there any new opportunities you can take advantage of? Are there any threats you need to be aware of? By asking yourself these questions, you can ensure that your value proposition is still relevant and attractive to your target market.

Next, examine your distribution channels. Are you using the right channels to reach your target market? Are there any new channels that you should be exploring? By staying up to date on new technologies and trends, you can find new ways to reach your customers and expand your business.

You should also analyze your revenue streams to ensure they are generating enough income to support your operations. Are there any new revenue streams you should be exploring? Are there any products or services you should be discontinuing? By reviewing your revenue streams, you can identify areas where you can increase profitability and growth potential.

Finally, evaluate your cost structure. Are your costs too high? Are there any areas where you can cut costs without sacrificing quality? By managing your costs effectively, you can ensure that your business remains profitable and sustainable in the long run.

Evaluating your business model regularly is essential for maximizing your business potential. By analyzing your value proposition, distribution channels, revenue streams, and cost structure, you can identify areas for improvement and growth. By staying up to date on new technologies and trends, you can ensure that your business remains relevant and competitive in the current market.

Developing a Winning Marketing Strategy

Marketing is one of the most critical aspects of running a successful business. Your marketing strategy influences how consumers view your brand and ultimately impacts your ability to acquire and retain customers. To develop a winning marketing strategy, you must first have a clear understanding of your target market. Who are they? What problems do they have that your product or service can solve?

Next, you must develop a brand persona that will resonate with your target market. This means identifying your brand's values, personality, and messaging. Your brand persona should reflect your target market's values and be consistent across all marketing channels, including social media, email marketing, and advertising.

Once you have identified your target market and crafted your brand persona, you can begin developing your marketing mix. Your marketing mix consists of the four Ps: product, price, place, and promotion. This framework helps ensure that all aspects of your marketing are aligned and working together to meet your business's overall goals.

When it comes to promotion, there are countless tactics you can use, from traditional advertising such as print and TV ads to more modern digital techniques like social media and influencer marketing. The key is to choose the tactics that will be most effective in reaching your target audience and conveying your brand persona.

Another critical aspect of marketing is tracking your results and adjusting your strategy accordingly. This means setting goals, tracking metrics such as website traffic and conversion rates, and using data to make informed decisions about future marketing investments.

Developing a winning marketing strategy requires a deep understanding of your target market, a well-crafted brand persona, a cohesive marketing mix, and a willingness to measure and adjust your approach as needed. With these elements in place, you can effectively reach and engage your target audience, helping to maximize your business's potential for success.

Creating a Productive Workspace

A productive workspace is essential for business success. Your workspace affects your work efficiency, creativity, and overall well-being. Creating a productive workspace requires more than just a desk and a chair. It requires thought and planning to design a space that promotes focus, quality work, and minimizes distractions.

The first step in creating a productive workspace is to declutter and organize. When you have a lot of things lying around, it can be difficult to concentrate, and it also makes it challenging to find the things you need. Get rid of anything that is no longer useful or doesn't inspire you. Keep your workspace clean, and put things away after using them.

The second step is to consider the ergonomics of your workspace. Your desk and chair should be comfortable and adjustable to prevent fatigue and injuries. Your computer screen should be at eye level, and your arms should rest comfortably on the desk.

The third step is to add personality to your workspace. You spend a significant portion of your day working, so it's essential to surround yourself with things that inspire and motivate you. You can add some plants, art, or anything that makes your workspace feel more comfortable and personalized.

The fourth step is to minimize distractions. It's easy to lose focus when you're constantly bombarded by emails, notifications, or other people's conversations. Try to eliminate these distractions by setting boundaries or using tools like noise-cancelling headphones or apps that block distracting websites.

The final step is to optimize your workspace for productivity. This means prioritizing the things that matter the most and making them easily accessible. Use tools like whiteboards, bulletin boards, or digital notepads to keep track of your to-do lists, deadlines, and ideas.

A productive workspace is crucial for business success. It requires thoughtful planning that includes decluttering, ergonomics, personalization, distraction minimization, and productivity optimization. By creating a workspace that promotes focus, quality work, and well-being, you're setting yourself up for success.

Leveraging Technology to Streamline Processes

Putting it All Together: Applying the Entrepreneurial Mindset
In today's digital age, technology is advancing at a rapid pace, and entrepreneurs who embrace this change can stay ahead of their competition. By leveraging the right technology, business owners can streamline processes that save time, increase productivity, and ultimately lead to increased profitability.

One of the primary benefits of technology is automation.

Automating repetitive, time-consuming tasks can free up valuable time and resources that can be better spent on other aspects of the business. For example, email marketing automation tools can automate the process of sending targeted emails based on customer behavior and preferences. Similarly, using project management tools can help in tracking progress and assigning tasks to team members.

Another way technology can streamline processes is by centralizing information. Using digital tools to store and access information can enhance collaboration within a team and ensure data accuracy. Cloud-based solutions can be extremely beneficial in this regard. For example, using OneDrive or Google Drive for storing and sharing files helps to keep everyone on the same page, regardless of their location.

Along with automating tasks and centralizing information, technology can also be used to streamline communication within an organization. Communication is critical in any business operation, and leveraging technology can help to ensure smooth communication among team members. Utilizing tools such as Skype, Slack, or Zoom can reduce the need for in-person meetings and help to cut down on time spent traveling to and from meetings.

Finally, automating customer relations management can be a game-changer for entrepreneurs. Keeping track of customer interactions, feedback, and support requests can be challenging, but with the right technology, managing the entire customer journey can be made more efficient. Using tools like Salesforce, Hubspot, or Intercom can help entrepreneurs to stay on top of customer interactions, enabling them to offer top-notch service and fulfillment.

Technology is a powerful tool for entrepreneurs looking to streamline their business processes, which can ultimately lead to increased profits and long-term stability. By embracing the latest advancements and leveraging the right technology, entrepreneurs can stay ahead of their competition and position themselves for success.

Investing in Yourself and Your Business

Continuing Education and Professional Development

Becoming an entrepreneur does not mean that you have to do everything by yourself. It's crucial to realize that you're not an authority in every aspect of business. There is always room to improve and strengthen your skills. That is where continuing education and professional development comes in.

Continuing education and professional development are ways to enhance your knowledge and remain competitive in the business sector. It involves broadening your knowledge base, refining your skills, and keeping up with trends and changes in the market.

There are many ways to continue your education and professional development. You can attend workshops, take courses, read books, stay up to date with industry journals, or take online classes. These avenues allow you to expand your knowledge, stay informed about emerging trends, and develop professionally.

One characteristic of any successful entrepreneur is that they keep the learning process rolling. Successful business owners understand the importance of keeping current on best practices, tools, and techniques that can help them improve their bottom line.

Make it a point to prioritize your continued education and professional development. Plan your schedule in advance, attend workshops and conferences that focus on your interests and needs, and cultivate ongoing relationships with experts in your field.

The business world is always evolving, and it's essential to keep up with changes in order to remain competitive. When you invest in yourself and continually expand your skill set, you position yourself for long-term success in the world of business.

Implementing Self-care Strategies

As an entrepreneur, it can be easy to get caught up in the hustle and bustle of building your business. You may find yourself working long hours and neglecting your personal wellbeing. However, it is important to remember that taking care of yourself is crucial to the success of your business.

One way to prioritize self-care is by implementing self-care strategies. This includes taking regular breaks, practicing mindfulness and meditation, exercising regularly and getting plenty of sleep. By doing so, you can maintain your physical and mental wellbeing, which will ultimately improve your productivity and performance.

Another important aspect of self-care is setting boundaries. This includes separating your work and personal life, and not allowing your business to take over your entire life. It's important to make time for your hobbies and interests outside of work, as this can help to reduce stress and improve your overall happiness.

Finally, don't be afraid to ask for help when you need it.

This includes delegating tasks to others on your team, seeking advice from mentors and peers, and taking advantage of resources that are available to you. Remember, no one can do it all on their own, and asking for help is a sign of strength, not weakness.

Implementing self-care strategies is crucial to the success of your business. By prioritizing your physical and mental wellbeing, setting boundaries and asking for help when needed, you can improve your productivity, reduce stress and ultimately build a successful business that you can be proud of.

Cultivating a Growth Mindset

Putting it All Together: Applying the Entrepreneurial Mindset

As an entrepreneur, having a growth mindset is critical to achieving business success. This mindset involves the belief that one's abilities and intelligence can be developed through hard work and dedication. It allows entrepreneurs to embrace challenges, learn from failures, and continually improve themselves and their businesses. Here are a few ways to cultivate a growth mindset:

Embrace Challenges: Rather than avoiding difficult tasks, embrace them as an opportunity to learn and grow. Don't be afraid to take on new projects or try new things.

Learn from Failure: Failure is an inevitable part of entrepreneurship, but it doesn't have to be a setback. Instead, view it as an opportunity to learn and improve. Analyze what went wrong, identify areas for improvement, and make changes accordingly.

Continually Seek Knowledge: Invest in ongoing learning, both personally and professionally. Attend conferences, read books, take courses or workshops, and seek out mentors and advisors.

Adopt a Positive Attitude: Believe in yourself and your abilities, and approach challenges with a positive mindset. Surround yourself with positive influences, and avoid negativity and self-doubt.

Practice Persistence: Building a successful business takes time, dedication, and persistence. Stay focused on your goals, and persevere through challenges and setbacks.

By cultivating a growth mindset, entrepreneurs can continually improve themselves and their businesses, and achieve long-term success.

Embracing Failure and Learning from Mistakes

Investing in Yourself and Your Business: Embracing Failure and Learning from Mistakes

As a budding entrepreneur, it's important to understand that failure is an inevitable part of the journey. In fact, it's often said that failure is a necessary component for success. Why? Because it provides valuable lessons and insights that you can use to make better decisions in the future, pivot when things are not working, or even take calculated risks more confidently.

Many successful entrepreneurs, like Pat Flynn, have had their fair share of failures, but have used these experiences to ultimately achieve success. The key is to not let failure define you, but instead see it as an opportunity to learn and grow.

One of the ways to embrace failure is to focus on small experiments and iterations. Don't put all your eggs in one basket, instead, try different things, test, and learn from what doesn't work. Incremental progress will lead to a deeper understanding of what works and what doesn't, thus minimizing the risks of bigger failure.

Another important mindset to adopt is reframing the concept of failure. Instead of seeing it as an end, see it as a stepping stone. Every mistake presents an opportunity to reflect on what went wrong, make adjustments, and move forward with new knowledge and insights.

Finally, it's important to recognize that failure is not the same as incompetence. One's ability to succeed or fail is not a reflection of their skills or intelligence, but instead a part of the entrepreneurial process. By embracing failure and learning from mistakes, you can use these as catalysts to achieve success and grow as a business owner.

Practicing Effective Time Management

Time is one of the most valuable resources an entrepreneur possesses. Learning how to effectively manage your time can make a significant difference in your level of productivity and success. Here are a few strategies to help you practice effective time management:

Set Clear Goals and Priorities: The first step in effective

time management is identifying your goals and prioritizing them. This includes short-term and long-term goals. Once you have clearly defined your goals, you can work backwards and create a schedule or timeline for achieving them.

Create a Daily Checklist: Creating a daily checklist or to-do list can help you stay on track with your goals and priorities. Be sure to include all of the tasks related to your business and personal life. Crossing off completed tasks can provide a sense of accomplishment and motivate you to keep going.

Eliminate Distractions: Distractions can seriously impede your ability to focus and get work done. Identify the biggest distractions that prevent you from being productive and take steps to eliminate them. This might include turning off your phone, closing your email inbox or finding a quiet workspace.

Delegate Tasks: As an entrepreneur, you may feel like you have to do everything yourself. However, delegating tasks to team members or outsourcing tasks can help you free up time and focus on the most important tasks. Prioritize tasks based on their importance and delegate accordingly.

Take Breaks: Remember to take breaks throughout the day to recharge and refresh your mind. This might include taking a walk, doing some stretching or simply taking a few deep breaths. Taking breaks can actually increase productivity by preventing burnout.

Evaluate and Refine Your Strategies: Finally, be sure to evaluate your time management strategies periodically and make adjustments as necessary. What works for one person may not work for another. Keep track of what tasks take up the most time and prioritize them accordingly.

By practicing effective time management, you can increase your productivity, reduce stress and achieve your goals more efficiently. Don't forget that time is a finite resource, so use it wisely!